Video Structure Meaning

Synthesis Lectures on Information Concepts, Retrieval, and Services

Editor

Gary Marchionini, *University of North Carolina at Chapel Hill*

Synthesis Lectures on Information Concepts, Retrieval, and Services publishes short books on topics pertaining to information science and applications of technology to information discovery, production, distribution, and management. Potential topics include: data models, indexing theory and algorithms, classification, information architecture, information economics, privacy and identity, scholarly communication, bibliometrics and webometrics, personal information management, human information behavior, digital libraries, archives and preservation, cultural informatics, information retrieval evaluation, data fusion, relevance feedback, recommendation systems, question answering, natural language processing for retrieval, text summarization, multimedia retrieval, multilingual retrieval, and exploratory search.

Video Structure Meaning
Brian C. O'Connor and Richard L. Anderson

ISBN: 978-3-031-01192-4   Paperback
ISBN: 978-3-031-02320-0   eBook
ISBN: 978-3-031-00227-4   Hardcover

DOI 10.1007/978-3-031-02320-0

A Publication in the Springer series
SYNTHESIS LECTURES ON INFORMATION CONCEPTS, RETRIEVAL, AND SERVICES
Lecture #68
Series Editor: Gary Marchionini, University of North Carolina, Chapel Hill

Series ISSN 1947-945X Print 1947-9468 Electronic

Video Structure Meaning

Brian C. O'Connor and Richard L. Anderson
The University of North Texas

SYNTHESIS LECTURES ON INFORMATION CONCEPTS, RETRIEVAL, AND SERVICES #68

ABSTRACT

For over a century, motion pictures have entertained us, occasionally educated us, and even served a few specialized fields of study. Now, however, with the precipitous drop in prices and increase in image quality, motion pictures are as widespread as paperback books and postcards once were. Yet, theories and practices of analysis for particular genres and analytical stances, definitions, concepts, and tools that span platforms have been wanting. Therefore, we developed a suite of tools to enable close structural analysis of the time-varying signal set of a movie. We take an information-theoretic approach (message is a signal set) generated (coded) under various antecedents (sent over some channel) decoded under some other set of antecedents. Cultural, technical, and personal antecedents might favor certain message-making systems over others. The same holds true at the recipient end—yet, the signal set remains the signal set.

In order to discover how movies work—their structure and meaning—we honed ways to provide pixel level analysis, forms of clustering, and precise descriptions of what parts of a signal influence viewer behavior. We assert that analysis of the signal set across the evolution of film—from Edison to Hollywood to Brakhage to cats on social media—yields a common ontology with instantiations (responses to changes in coding and decoding antecedents).

KEYWORDS

computational film analysis, video structure, functional ontology, photons in and out

Contents

The dominant, all-powerful factor of the film image is rhythm, expressing the course of time within the frame.

Andrey Tarkovsky, *Sculpting in Time*

Shot and montage are the basic elements of cinema. Montage has been established by the Soviet film as the nerve of cinema. To determine the nature of montage is to solve the specific problem of cinema.

Sergei Eisenstein, *A Dialectic Approach to Film Form*, in *Film Form*

Preface

While we come from different generations, we both have long been immersed in film and have both long pondered how the structure of a signal influences any recipient of that signal—that is, what does it mean to the recipient. Those streams of thought and experimentation came together nearly two decades ago and have continued to bolster some of our early thoughts, yield intriguing syntheses, and urge our deeper explorations. This is a biography of a model.

While we refer to some work by others and reference some work of significance, we do not present a broad introduction to theories of video and meaning; having early on found most of the work based in literary theory to be of little help in understanding film, we began from scratch—from the practices of filmmakers, from forms of examination newly available in the digital era, and from comparing our experiments with expert analyses. It is our hope to provoke fruitful critiques and even deeper examination in new directions by others.

There are many streams of influence and investigation at play. We tell our story in a manner influenced by our colleague, philosopher Irene Klaver (2018) who says of meandering:

> From early modernity onward, meanders were engineered away to facilitate modern developments, such as commercial river transportation, property boundary determinations, and city planning. Meandering proceeds covering more ground, percolating into deeper depths, listening to more voices, foregrounding the specificity of being what it is when and where it is observed. Meandering makes room for the slow and for the workings of the material realm not ruled by strict structures. It facilitates a slow ontology [and] a slow epistemology.

Meandering is a model for our decades of exploration of the structure of movies: working with a colleague on a project and returning five years later to work together on another phase; wrestling with ideas here, being inspired by a conversation there; enabling the convention of saying "we," even when chronology does not hold particular colleagues to us at a particular time. Because film is a mode of communication fundamentally different than verbal documents and because our research is the result of deep personal engagement with image making, when we present our work in person, we relate elements of that engagement. When we present our work in lectures, we generally cast our thoughts and constructs in filmic form of one sort or another, so we embark on our meandering with an introduction in the form of a movie trailer and origin stories to establish the depth of immersion in film and video structure.

We hope to provoke new takes on our model, different avenues of exploration, and a shared passion for moving image documents.

A word about this text is in order. For many years, we have given lectures and made conference presentations together in a conversational style and replicate that approach herein. This may seem odd or even like a "postmodern pastiche of personal narrative, memoir, and shot sheet" as an anonymous reviewer commented. That is intentional. We are of two different generations and come from radically different backgrounds; yet, we share a passion for film and for bringing information to the point of use. The personal narrative relates the development of an understanding of filmic structure from the early days and through personal engagement with the medium. The threads woven into this biography of a model may, in themselves, provide a clue for a reader to some other deeper understanding.

Acknowledgments

We owe a great deal of thanks to the many people who inspired, nudged, critiqued, and tolerated us during this project, especially Roger Wyatt, Irene Klaver, Melody McCotter, Ethan O'Connor, Jodi Kearns, Barbra and Richard Anderson, Diane Cerra, and our colleagues and students in the Visual Thinking Laboratory in the College of Information at the University of North Texas. We thank series editor Gary Marchionini, who has long conducted and supported research on video and meaning.

We would especially like to acknowledge Bertrand Augst for his utter passion for film, his inspiration, and his decades of deep commitment to understanding cinema and culture.

CHAPTER 1

Introduction

1.1 TRAILER: MOVIES AS STRUCTURED COLLECTIONS OF PHOTOGRAPHS

Movies arose from a history of entertainment, engineering, and science. They also arose from still pictures. In fact, a movie is nothing more (or less) than a sequence of still images with one primary structuring attribute—presentation of the set of still images to the viewer at a fixed rate. For the video media available these days that rate is 30 frames per second. So, every minute of viewing time is made up of 1,800 still images. What can we say about these collections of images that helps us understand how they function for viewers, and how they generate meaning?

Figure 1.1: Individual frames samples from seven seconds of video.

There are no restrictions as to what those frames should be for any given video, only that they should be presented at 30 frames per second if the illusion of life-like motion is to be maintained. Simply giving a viewer a package of 1,800 still images would not result in an illusion of motion. In order to be a movie, the images must be structured in such a way as to be presentable at 30 frames per second. Figure 1.2 presents a portion of the frames from a Hollywood movie printed at approximately the size of the original frames. More than 12,000 frames from a 7-minute section of the movie are printed on a large sheet of paper. They make for a nice poster and they are not without use, but they are not a movie.

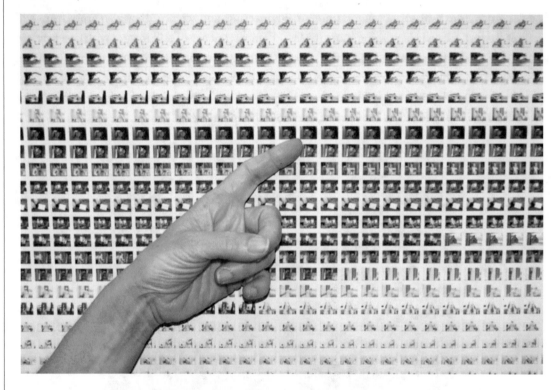

Figure 1.2: Mural print of more than 12,000 frames from a seven-minute portion of *The Birds* (author's photo).

Whether the recording device is a film camera, an analog video camera, or a digital video camera, it is a device that records many still images rapidly. It is not a device that records motion. It is a device that records fragments of motion. In fact, there is a significant amount of time in which it is not recording anything, even when running.

That is to say, this sort of collection of images functions as a movie, if and only if playback is made at the prescribed frame rate. The structural element is temporal. Now, this is not to say that the collection cannot be used in other ways. Football coaches have made a significantly different use of movies for decades by violating the temporal element. Stopping a film at the moment a particularly good or bad move was recorded, reversing the film and playing a short sequence over again and again, or fast-forwarding through portions that are not relevant for the particular segment of the team watching the film. Police, athletic coaches, and film theorists all routinely look at some portions of film or video footage in slow motion or even frame-by-frame looking for a particular momentary piece of data or a particular discontinuity in the data. High-speed recording of numerous frames (perhaps hundreds or even thousands of frames per second) enables playback at very slow motion and, thus, analysis of a large number of data points per second.

On the whole, the filmic collection of frames is structured such that it only functions when played back at a standard rate.

When we say "function," we mean act as a message as generated by an author/videomaker. Whether the individual viewer understands the message in the same way as intended by the author is a separate issue from transmission of the message. The meaning of the video message to a recipient, what it puts into the viewer's mind, what it enables the viewer to do is a decoding process, just as the message making is a coding process.

How are we to find and make sense and make use of filmic documents? Let us think about the production and viewing processes to see if we can tease out other structures. Let us look briefly at the film construction process, then at the film viewing process. Here we will use the example of a documentary film on a rodeo, as at the left. There is no particular reason for this choice, except that documentaries generally fall between the individually produced home movie or artistic piece and the large production team construction of a Hollywood feature.

We make use of the term "photocutionary acts" as modeled by Greisdorf and O'Connor (2008) on Austin's "illocutionary acts" for speech acts, performative utterances—"to say something is to do something" (Austin, 1976). We take this to be the doing of something with photographs (stills and filmic) regardless of the formality of the purpose or production process.

The filmmaker engages in one or more photocutionary acts. Either by pre-planning or by making decisions at the moment of recording, the filmmaker gathers together a collection of images at the rodeo. The content of those images—both topic and production values—will have been guided by the filmmaker's plan for the collection, as well as by the filmmaker's understanding of the intended audience. That is, if the filmmaker wants to present the human athletic ability of rodeo riders, then the majority of images in the collection will be constructed to give more frame space to the riders than to horses, clowns, or audience. If, on the other hand, the filmmaker intends an ethnographic study of the rituals surrounding rodeo, then there likely will be many images showing behind the scenes preparations, audience members reacting to events, announcers, clowns, and all the other participants.

After all the images have been made, they will be arranged. Some of the original images will likely be discarded for poor technical quality, duplication, lack of appropriateness for the film, length considerations, or any myriad of other artistic and logistical reasons. The filmmaker may choose to leave the images in more or less chronological order or to re-arrange the images to suit the plan of the film.

There is no "grammar" of film in the sense of a verbal grammar. There is no analog to the noun or verb. This does not mean that there are no structures to movies, far from it. However, the structures are built on the understanding of viewer perception. Filmmakers learned long ago that structure is a powerful component; they also learned that there is no one-to-one correspondence of filmic structural practices to verbal practices. There are some "tried and true" practices, such as using "fast" editing to increase excitement. However, there are other methods of achieving excitement and the rapid intercutting of dull or inappropriate images will not achieve excitement.

So, the filmmaker carries out photocutionary acts at the image gathering and image ordering stages. In a general sense, the filmmaker also conducts photocutionary acts at the showing stage by determining the type of recording and distribution mechanisms (e.g., wide release in theaters, showing to a few friends, releasing direct to DVD, etc.) Likewise, the viewer carries out several photocutionary acts. The most evident is the choice to view a particular work. Once upon a time, the collection of movies was limited to whatever came to the local theater. Film viewing was passive at many levels, not the least of which was that the collection came in bits and pieces and did not accumulate (the reels for last week's film were on their way to another town.) In some communities, public libraries had small collections of films, generally of the sort used in schools, but that was really the extent if it. Now, of course, it is quite the opposite. Between multiplex theaters in most municipalities, multiple video rental outlets, cable television, video-on-demand, video on the web, and video on numerous personal portable devices the collection of videos is enormous and is no longer ephemeral. So, simply choosing a movie document is now an active photocutionary act.

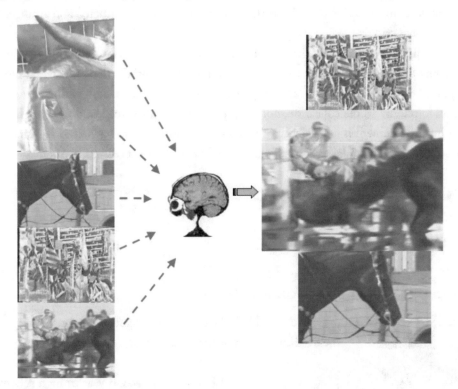

In the past, watching a movie in a theater or a television show at home was a passive experience in which the images went by in their prescribed order and at the prescribed rate. When the movie ended, that was the end of the viewing act unless one paid for another viewing or waited for re-runs. Now re-runs are easier to find and there is a large array of time-shifting devices and practices. There is also the ability to directly and actively engage in the viewing process. The ability to rewind, speed ahead, and play one segment over and over is now no longer only available to producers and a few privileged users (e.g., athletic coaches, law enforcement, scientists) whose work enabled them to purchase expensive playback machinery. Videotape, then various digital media, have made it possible for virtually any user to view the collection of still images making up the movie in almost any manner they like. For the majority of situations the standard playback rate is still the default mode, but examination and re-examination of individual frames and sets of frames is not only possible but also essentially trivial to achieve.

In either case, simple passive viewing or highly interactive viewing, it is the case that photocutionary acts are taking place. In the passive, single viewing it is unlikely that most viewers of a half-hour documentary or a two-hour feature film will recall every image in its prescribed order. Some images will be more striking and more memorable; some will be remembered out of context or out of order; some will likely be misremembered. After the viewing, there will be, in effect, another collection of images. This one will be the viewer's collection, constructed and arranged by the viewer's individual criteria.

So we might say of a movie that it is, in the most general model, a collection of still images structured first and foremost by the mechanical necessities of reproduction. The actual number of still images is large—1,800 frames per minute of viewing time. Ordinarily, a viewer comes to such a collection to see the whole collection, not simply a few particular images. So, we might say that a moving image document is a collection of images that is intended to be viewed as a single document, so it pushes the boundaries of the definition of a collection—a collection of one.

1.2   ORIGIN STORIES

1.2.1   BRIAN MISE EN SCÈNE

Mise en Scène 1: 1962 in a high school football team meeting room

Coach Hall: "Jack, see how he gets a step on you right there?! Run the projector back and go slow motion …stop! See? Right there."

In 1962 I was in my second year of high school when Coach Hall came to me with a Bolex 16 mm movie camera and asked if I could figure out how to make it work and make some game films for the team to study. I was an avid photographer and I had a library card, so I said "Yes, sir!" Pointing the camera, pushing the motor button, and even developing a short test roll of film were all quite like making still pictures. In fact, it was making still pictures, lots of them!

The best films ever taken of a game are of little value if the coach can't properly analyze them because his projector is not adapted to this sort of work.

The school's sound projectors are just not designed for this job. A specially constructed projector is needed, one that is rugged enough to withstand the hard abuse it receives during the season

Figure 1.3: Quote from *How to Make Good Coaching Movies* (Kodak, 1964) with inset photo of Brian.

In the first team meeting where we watched the first game film, I was fascinated, almost shocked. The projector could stop the film and hold a single frame on the screen, it could run forward and reverse, and the speed could be slowed to about half normal speed. I had been "projector boy" in school for many years, so I was quite accustomed to movies, yet they had always been shown in school just as in the theater and on television—the movie started and played to the end without stopping. The audience experience was one of passive viewing. The football coaching film was interactive—under the control of the viewer.

Structure of the actual film document was significant and quite different from movies and TV shows of the day. An entire game was represented on roughly 12 minutes of film. There was no audio because there was no need for it for coaching; only the time from the snap of the ball until the paly was whistled dead was recorded. As Coach Hall said: "No cheerleaders, no close shots, no band—only plays!" The coaching function only required the plays and would have been hampered by any additional material, no matter how entertaining or artistic. The structure of the coaching film was imposed at two significant points: during the actual recording of the game and dynamically during the coaching session viewings. Both points of structuring were critical to the meaning of the film. The meaning of the film was to present good and bad moves by the players and enable incremental and repeatable presentation essentially step-by-step, literally. The meaning for the players was becoming better at their sport. Very simple structure of images combined with re-structuring enabled by slow motion and multiple viewings yielded meaning for coaches and players

Nowadays, almost anyone can pick up smartphone or a tablet and view games or individual plays in the palm of the hand; the mechanisms of viewing have almost completely dissolved. Yet, it remains the case that moving pictures of any sort are made up of still photographs, lots of them.

Silent 16 mm film was often shot at just about the threshold for the illusion of motion to avoid frequent reloading of the camera and to save some money for the high school; 16 mm film with sound was shot at somewhat higher speed because of the mechanics of the sound system; digital video is generally shot at a little higher rate. Thus, every minute of silent 16 mm requires 1,080 still photographs; every minute of sound 16 mm requires; and every minute of digital video requires 1,800 still photographs.

Figure 1.4: Analog viewing mechanism and digital viewing mechanism.

It would be hard to overstate the impact of mechanism on the functionality of motion pictures in the analog era, on representation for access and analysis, and so, on meaning.

Mise en Scène 2: A class of six undergraduate students studying the Roman poet Catullus

In 1966 I was studying Greek and Latin literature and dabbling in the very early days of programming in BASIC (Beginner's All-purpose Symbolic Instruction Code) and spending a great deal of time in the film society and the local movie theater. Discussing Catullus we compared his brief poems with the epic heroic tales of the canon, especially Vergil's Aeneid. Where Vergil sang of gods and heroes, Catullus wrote of his love for a woman and things in daily life that caught his attention; where Vergil used 9,896 lines for his great work, Catullus used only 2 for one of his greatest works; where Vergil used dactylic hexameter, Catullus crafted his two-line piece as an elegiac couplet, in which the use of individual letters literally embodied the anguished passion when the lines were spoken. Here was the beginning of my understanding of crafting meaning with more than words and rules of grammar.

Not long afterward I had the opportunity to participate in some of the early computational analysis of Greek and Latin works in the days of punched paper tape and punched 80 column cards. What was fascinating to me in this was the use of the blank space as a way of marking where clumps of letters were bounded, together with the notion that each character—letters, other marks, and even blank spaces each had an address in the document.

Of more significance than I would know for some time, I watched the films of, listened to, and worked for one afternoon with experimental film luminary Stan Brakhage. His work seemed to me quite like that of Catullus, for it was terse, personal, and highly worked at the frame level to express notions beyond linear narrative. This culminated in a senior project in which I argued that Catullus and other neoteric poets stood in relation to Vergil in much the same way that the experimental film artists of the 1940s–1960s stood to Hollywood. The descriptive prose of the piece was sufficient to make the primary argument, yet I had not been able to make the argument in terms of the poetry and the film styles. The tools existed for analyzing the poetry, but not for the films.

Mise en Scène 3: Immersion in structure

A decrepit neighborhood with roach-infested, crumbling rental properties—walking with residents to document conditions for a program sponsored by a War on Poverty agency. How could we present an emotional hook for the report of statistics and graphs in a paper report prepared by the same agency? A 30-minute collage of exterior and interior images with a soundtrack collage of voices of residents with no "expert" narrator (the residents were the experts of their own lives) emerged and played widely on television, in a U.S. Senate committee, and as a training film for VISTA volunteers.

Film editing studio in a university art department—working on a graduate degree in film I viewed classic works of documentary and experimental films over and over while planning my portfolio films. Immersion in the documentary and art film worlds of the New York City area meant proximity to filmmakers and their explanations of why they did what they did; as well profound critiques of my own experiments. HP and Riefenstahl—Canyon Cinema 24,000 views on YouTube.

Federal Reserve Ninth District headquarters in Minneapolis—how to design a 30-minute film on the workings of the Fed 200 hours—3 hours—10 days; 30 minute—6 months. 199 hours into the dumpster.

Mise en Scène 4: Filmic representation

Engagement with film meandered from production of documentary and art films to graduate studies at UC Berkeley, working on film and representation.

Revisions to the Anglo-American Cataloguing Rules were underway at the time. Reading through the proposed rules for cataloging photographs, I was astonished that the notions presented had little to do with the ways in which photographers, editors, advertisers, and others who worked with photographs spoke of the or used them. Theodora Hodges, asked if I would care to write a paper on my concerns— "Access to Images: Axes to Grind." It was here that the idea of using production concepts and expertise as a foundation for modeling and representing movies began.

In 1981, film theorist and member of the Berkeley Comparative Literature faculty Bertrand Augst asked me: "Why can't we use a computer to measure and speak of filmic structure in the same way we can for a verbal text?" He had conducted computational analysis of French literature in the 1960s, so this was an obvious question. The primary answer was that there was not yet any available system for digitizing. So we worked on modeling film in hopes of making some progress so as to be ready when digitizing became available. We dropped the literary metaphor and devised a time-varying signal set model.

During my research I still showed my films in classes and in venues such as Canyon Cinema. My portfolio film on horse pulling generated reactions that provided an informal data set on structure and meaning. As one might expect, the topic brought out a mix of reactions, but more intriguing was the near even divide among viewers over the structure. The film is a seven-minute visual poem about an event I had attended since early childhood, so I made it an impression of images and sounds. There is no explanation of what is happening and only the intriguing, dancerly movements of the horses and drivers are shown most all of the ordinary explanatory objects and events are not shown. Also, the camera is always very close to the horses and drivers. Some people "loved" the "abstractness," while others "hated" that they couldn't "tell what was going on"; likewise, some "loved" being "so close to the action, like I am in the ring," while a near equal number "hated" the "claustrophobia."

Working with information philosopher Patrick Wilson, I formalized my explorations into a dissertation on film and representation—how does film represent the world and how might we represent film in such a way as to make it a tool with utility analogous to books and journal articles. We might re-state this as looking at how film structures time and space and how might we use this understanding to generate topographic maps of films to enable control over locus and depth of penetration into a filmic text.

1.2.2   RICH MISE EN SCÈNE

Mise en Scène 5: Massaman Curry and Garlic Tofu

My entry into the field of film analysis is somewhat serendipitous. I was a doctoral student on the cusp of a dissertation proposal. I had come into information science from the field of Behavior

Analysis. My day job at the time involved managing the cybersecurity program for a large university. I was hoping to write a dissertation that involved these two fields.

On the night my career in film analysis began, I was having dinner with Brian to discuss some barriers and frustrations I was having with my dissertation. First, I discovered that another researcher in the cybersecurity field who was farther along with his dissertation than I was had independently pursued a similar idea. Second, I had encountered some bureaucratic resistance to the idea of using real world cybersecurity data for my research. All in all, this was a distressing state of affairs.

Our dinner arrived, garlic tofu for Brian and massaman curry for me. Over the course of dinner, our conversation shifted from the specific problem I was working, finding an effective way of visualizing and communicating complex and high volume security data (such as that produced by network intrusion detection systems) to decision makers who likely did not have domain expertise, to the theoretical underpinnings of my dissertation. The general idea was to transform the data in a way that the consumer of the data could see everything at once and apply stimulus control principles to draw their attention to the areas that needed attention.

As conversations tend to do, we moved from my dissertation to a problem that Brian had been working on with his mentor, Betrand Augst. Augst had been interested for some time in analyzing film using computers much in the same way textual documents had been analyzed. Augst thought the work of Raymond Bellour provided a potential framework for computation film analysis. In "System of a Fragment," Bellour provided a detailed and rigorous analysis of the Bodega Bay sequence of Alfred Hitchcock's *The Birds*. As Brian and I finished dinner, we realized that we could conduct a functional analysis of Bellour's work and develop a computer-based heuristic for analyzing film with modern technology.

A few days later, we printed 12,084 frames from the Bodega Bay sequence of *The Birds* on a 9'×4' color print and hung it on the wall. It did not take long to identify the significant discontinuities in the data that correlated with Bellour's analysis of the same data. In October of that year, Brian and I presented our initial work at the Document Academy in Berkeley, CA and had the opportunity to meet with Bertrand Augst, describe our work, and show off our 9'×4' print of the frames.

Over coffee, I described my approach as "tear apart to reveal structure; deconstruct and synthesize." My dissertation came about a year later and we have used the general ideas first discussed over massaman curry and garlic tofu to create the research described in this volume.

CHAPTER 2

Five Stories to a Model of Video Structure

2.1 STORY ONE: MIRROR WITH A MEMORY

2.1.1 JUST WHAT IS A PHOTOGRAPH?

Since a moving picture document is a set of still photographs, we want to consider in some depth just what sort of document a photograph is. In 2009, we were working on a project with imaging engineer Ethan O'Connor for a presentation on ultra-high resolution photography of museum objects; we constructed the following considerations and model. Note that it was Ethan who commented: "All of photography can be summed up as photons in, photons out."

In June of 1859, physician, essayist, and photographer Oliver Wendell Holmes (1859) (pictured at the right) wrote in the *Atlantic Monthly* that photography provided humans a "mirror with a memory." We could have direct, indexical representations of the world about us that would remain fixed across space and time. We have 5,000 years of practice thinking with words but scarcely a century and a half of practice thinking with pictures, both still and moving. Now that the means of production and viewing are simple and controllable, we find ourselves able to practice new ways of thinking in, with, and about video. Plato argued that words were useful because they were stripped of specificity; Holmes argued (as do we) that images are useful precisely because of their specificity. Videos return us to the specificity of lived life.

Oliver Wendell Holmes, 1859

Let us consider pictures. Or, rather, let us consider photography. Or, perhaps more usefully, let us consider acts that we characterize as photography. We assert: Photography = Light goes in, then Light comes out. More specifically, information about the photons present in a region of space and region of time is in some way carried through time or space and allowed to "live again" in a manner that exceeds our expectations for how light behaves when it is not manipulated.

So, what traits does a photon have? Direction of travel, location, wavelength (polarity too…), intensity/flux, and its variation with time and space. The manner in which these characteristics are mapped from the input photons and light volume to the output photons and light volume encompasses the entirety of photography.

If we think about photons, we realize that they come from some place at some time and in the making of a photograph they (or their lineage) present a past state of affairs. We might then propose that photographs and perhaps documents in general are mechanisms that resolve the past or predict the future in a universe that makes both acts seemingly impossible.

Another way to think of a document is to ask what sort of resolving power does a document afford one in determining a past state? A photographic document presents a means of recovering the vector state of the past that is more useful—enables a closer mapping—in some situations. There exists the possibility of recovering from the initial files, the temporal, spatial, and spectral component(s) of some State 1 from the State 2 represented in the photograph. As one possible example, consider the word "greave." For most people today this is not a sufficiently common entity in daily life for the single word to bring to mind or use, say, the three-dimensional shape of the entity. Even a passage from Homer may not be sufficient to do so:

> As he spoke his strong hand hurled his javelin from him, and the spear struck Achilles on the leg beneath the knee; the greave (κνημίς) of newly wrought tin rang loudly, but the spear recoiled from the body of him whom it had struck, and did not pierce it, for the gods gift stayed it. (616).

> Homer, *The Iliad* (ed. Samuel Butler) book 21, line 590.

It would perhaps make more sense for the modern reader to use the translation "shin guard."

A standard two-dimensional photograph may present a closer mapping between the document and the original entity or state. Stereographs from the nineteenth century and various three-dimensional imaging systems today are capable of even closer mapping between State 1 and State 2. There is, of course, a wrinkle in our representation. The photograph is not from the time of Homer; rather, it is from a modern reproduction of a Homeric tale. The greaves in the movie were constructed by one-to-one mapping from ancient greaves to modern reproductions—in themselves, then, a form of document.

We have photographs of gullies on Mars. Gullies on Mars are not coded by humans. They exist as the result of laws of physics operating over time. Humans participate in coding by lens design, sensor design, transmission system design, and target selection. Photographs of gullies on Mars are like snapshots of a birthday party—both record surface structures for future use.

A photograph made of a butterfly on a planet in the Vega star system would not be a document on Earth because it would be too far away to interact with an entity on Earth. Even if residents of Earth had received a notice that a photograph would be made on some particular date at a Vega butterfly colony and sent at the speed of light on that date toward Earth, it could have no impact on an Earth resident for about 25.3 years. Now, it might be argued that knowing a Vega butterfly image was on its way might impact an Earth resident, but that impact would be only from the initial notice that such an image would someday be on the way.

2.1.2   PHOTONS IN, PHOTONS OUT

Our consideration of the movement, capture, and display of photons leads us to modeling photocutionary acts and how we might think of them as resolving the past. During the pre-capture of data stage, decisions are made about just where to aim the capture devise, what sort of time frame would be appropriate for the capture, whether the capture should be artless or artful—here think of NASA high-resolution imaging of shuttle parts to look for stress fractures vs. gauze filters to smooth imperfections in a "romantic" portrait—and issues of lighting. At the capture stage the mechanics of what sort of lens would be ideal (focal length, maximum aperture, linear distortions, chromatic distortions, price, and time required) are combined with determining tradeoffs of expense, rigging, intrusion on the subject (one would likely not set up a high-resolution imaging system that requires a five-minute exposure to record a child's birthday party; nor would one propose making official museum records of holdings with a cell phone camera.)

At the post-capture stage issues of changing brightness, tone curves, contrast, filtering, and numerous other manipulations are weighed against issues of verisimilitude: legs made "perfect" for an advertising campaign by lengthening; eliminating distracting elements from a cover photo for a national magazine; Photoshopping out a piece of lettuce in the smile of a faculty website portrait. At the publication stage technical decisions about the quality of printing, color management, storage space, and simple size of the displayed image are weighed against issues of utility, cost-to-gain ratios (a 3 × 12 foot print of the Very Large Array might be the perfect image to enhance a conference room, but the several hundred dollar cost of just mounting the print, instead of tacking it to the wall, is not trivial.) Re-use of images raises issues of whether they ought to be displayed in a different size or format than originally intended. We might ask if display of a digital version of an antique photograph "violates" original intentions. We might ask if a "better" print serves some purposes well, while casting a curtain between the image and what earlier viewers would have experienced.

This line of reasoning yields a model of relationships. This model is a demonstration from which to conduct discussions and elaborations. Source of photons may be taken as State 1; capture as State 2; each post-production editing step as Stage 3a, 3b, 3c …; each display decision or instantiation as Stage 4a, 4b, 4c, …; each access/retrieval decision as 5a, 5b, 5c, …; each re-use activity as 6a, 6b, 6c… We might add that agents at each stage might actively want to know the mechanical and / or the human decision components of previous photocutionary acts. We might note that this wave of coherence through time is instantiated in what would look like individual documents, so we might want to consider Anderson's notion of document lineages (O'Connor, Anderson, and Kearns, 2008, p. 38.)

We describe this trail of the rules for recovery of the past as a "chain of custody"—familiar from archival science and criminal investigations for assuring provenance and protection from fraud. It is conceptually simple, though tracking the human decision making may not be so simple. At every stage each photocutionary act has a mechanical and decisional component.

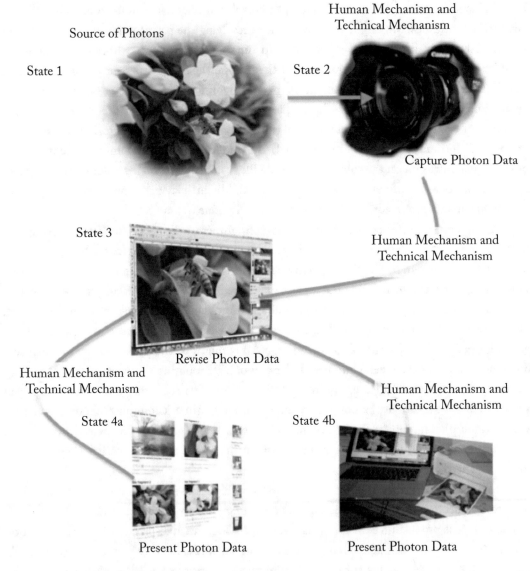

Figure 2.1: Photons in, photons out: photographic chain of custody.

We offer this model as a substructure for discussing photocutionary acts with the rigor that has long been available for word documents. Among the myriad of questions at play we have the following.

- How are we to envision the boundary between image-as-bits and image-as-photons?

- How do we speak of photon metadata—or do we?

- Can we/ought we to extract information beyond photographers' intent?

- Are there meaningful differences between measuring, reproducing, expressing, …?

2.2   STORY TWO: FIRST STEPS

The pertinent portion of Brian's doctoral research was concerned with the making of abstracts [being] primarily a matter of generating surrogates which will represent the differences in structure and extra-topical aspects of film and video works by which a user might make a relevance judgment either during browsing or during inspection of a group of documents supplied by a retrieval system. A summary of that thinking, derived from my article (O'Connor, 1985) follows.

2.2.1   BACKGROUND

The film or tape document is only an intermediate step, much like a computer program, for the repeatable generation of a text. Light or electromagnetic radiation is modulated by the encoding apparatus onto the substrate, producing a text which Augst (1980a) notes is: "un-attainable, in the sense first used by Bellour of *introuvable*, by being literally and figuratively unquotable, everlastingly slipping through in the instance of being identified, seized for closer scrutiny."

Conceptualizing information as a complex relationship between societal and idiosyncratic conventions of sender and receiver and medium, which changes an individual's internal representations of the world argues, as Maron (1982) suggests: "The function of the document retrieval system cannot be to retrieve all and only the relevant documents … because the system does not know which are the relevant documents—that information simply does not exist."

2.2.2   INADEQUACY OF CURRENT ACCESS TOOLS

Broadly speaking, words are general signs connected by convention to a concept, and made more specific by syntax, whereas pictures are specific and made general by their context (in the moving image document this would largely be juxtaposition with other images), which acts according to Pryluck (1976) to "reduce unique attributes of an object to general attributes of a class of objects". The two sources of meaning in an image document can be seen as the object or event recorded and the way in which it is presented. Pryluck (1976) also notes that the variety of recording and post-production elements "emphasize or obscure some attributes of the object, thus affecting the meaning consequent on the attributes of an object."

Words and photographic images can be seen as two regions on a spectrum of modes of symbolic description with very little in common. Pryluck (1976) assertss: "In an attempt to identify those characteristics which are common to the sign systems and those which are unique ... beyond the fact that both language and image communication mediate experience for recipients, few common characteristics were identified. The structures of language and image communication were found to differ in almost every detail."

Novitz (1977) and Pryluck (1976) point out that pictures are specifically related to a particular object or event, whereas a word is general and refers, in Pryluck's words "to a set of critical attributes, but says nothing of other attributes which may be crucial to some meaning of the object." By making changes in the image coding variables one can reduce or enhance the "unique attributes of an object" and thereby control the degree of generalization.

Metz (1974), in a similar vein, focuses on the primary differences between words and moving image "shots".

1. Shots are infinite in number, contrary to words, but like statements, which can be formulated in a verbal language.

2. Shots are the creations of the film-maker, unlike words (which pre-exist in lexicons) but similar to statements (which are, in principle, the invention of the speaker).

3. The shot presents the receiver with a quantity of undefined information, contrary to the word. From this viewpoint, the shot is not even equivalent to the sentence. Rather, it is like the complex statement of undefined length.

4. The shot is an actualized unit, a unit of discourse, an assertion, unlike the word (which is purely a lexical unit), but like a statement, which always refers to reality. [

The meaning of two or more shots put together can be quite different from that of the individual shots (the "third" effect); viewer perception of the same shot can be quite different when it is put together with different shots (Kuleshov effect); timing and ordering of shots can affect perceived meaning. Worth (1981) defines "sequence"as "a deliberately employed series used for the purpose of giving meaning rather than order to more than one image-event and having the property of conveying meaning through the sequence itself as well as through the elements in the sequence".

Pryluck, Teddlie, and Sands (1982) used an "image-based" and non-verbal procedure to examine the "construction of meaning from sequenced images" and concluded:

"The evidence is clear that the production variables (order and time) and the event variable (set ambiguity) affect the interpretation of a set of images. Equally clear is the evidence that these are interacting variables. We are dealing with a complex, dynamic phenomenon that will not be simply explained."

2.2.3   ELEMENTS FOR A SURROGATE

The description of the physical document must accommodate the variety of horizontal and vertical juxtapositions of portions of the image and sound tracks that characterize the moving image text; it must make available those elements and relationships that are not available to the user by unmediated inspection of the physical documents. Previous considerations of topic, conventions, text, and users have indicated that the meaning of a text is the result of a number of variables that in Watt's (1979) terms "reside in both the audience and the medium."

Peritore (1977) and Yamaguchi (1982) assert that a surrogate for a moving image document must include a description of both the objects recorded and the depiction variables; that is, it must account for the distinction between the physical document and the topic and the interaction between the two. There are many variables subject to manipulation. Documents may range from mere recordings of objects or events to those in which the meaning is derived from elaborate manipulations. The description of the physical text must accommodate the variety of horizontal and vertical juxtapositions of portions of the image and sound tracks which characterize the moving image text; it must make available those elements and relationships which are not available to the user by unmediated inspection of the physical documents. The nature of images may make difficult, if not impossible, the complete elaboration of relationships which might be of interest.

Nichols (1982) addresses the difficulty of using words to describe photographs: "As a consequence of this difference between analogue [pictures] and digital [words] we are often in the position ... of describing gradations of meaning with obviously crude instruments such as the distinctions background/foreground, diagonal/vertical, black/white, close-up/medium shot/long shot." The meaningfulness, the rhetorical force, and the propositional capabilities are dependent on the codes of depiction as well as on the objects on the picture and sound tracks.

For the purposes of a base-level description, a moving image document can be visualized as a matrix of several sequential phenomena. The vertical axis is composed of rows for the image and sound tracks—typically, but not necessarily, one image, synchronized voice, synchronized effects, voice-over narration or commentary, music, non-synchronized voices, and effects. The horizontal axis is a timeline with column increments the size of the frame in the recording medium (now generally 1/24th or 1/30th of a second). This provides a reference structure for describing what takes place at any moment within any one of the tracks, and, thus, what relationships hold vertically between combinations of tracks, as well as what sorts of relationships hold within a single track. Thus, for example, lengths of shots (edemes) and points at which they change may be noted; the amount or percentage of time given to music or narration may be calculated; or the use of one or more sound tracks to bridge a picture transition may be described. In order to describe a document more is required than the ability to describe when portions of tracks begin and end; description of what objects appear, what they do, and what depiction variables are being applied or manipulated is required. This may be accomplished by sub-dividing the description of the tracks, so that each includes:

1. a description of the object-event under consideration;

2. a description of the relationship of the object-event to the frame lines;

3. a description of the recording devices and the ways in which they relate to or present the object-event; and

4. a description of time-both movements of objects and recording devices, as well as lengths and juxtapositions of portions of tracks.

The selection of keywords or the generation of abstracts from print linguistic texts is hardly a simple matter; the difficulty of selecting portions of a moving image work is compounded by differences between words and moving images noted above. Essentially, there is no easily defined unit of meaning and there is no systematic, broadly applied grammar.

The "shot" is the common production and analysis unit; it is made up of a number of frames. In the text as viewed, a change of shot generally presents a change of viewpoint or a change of object photographed, as if the camera had been turned off, moved, and turned on again. However, objects may move and the camera may move, so that it is possible for a change of object or viewpoint to take place without the camera being stopped. Similarly, it is possible for the transition between two shots to be virtually unnoticed, so that the two seem as one. For some purposes the film or tape as recorded is acceptable or preferred; for other purposes necessity or intentions require that pieces of the original material be shortened, rearranged, joined with pieces from another recording, or otherwise manipulated. Thus it must be asked: What is meant by unit? What number of frames makes up a shot? Frames from which part of the production process were utilized?

Considerable attention was given to the shot by those such as Worth and Metz who attempted to apply linguistic methods to the film communication process in search of the "language of film," and found both the phrase and the linguistic model wanting. Worth (1981), in his "vidistic" enquiry, isolated the "shot" as the smallest unit of film that a filmmaker uses and termed it "videme." Yet a greater degree of precision was required in order to account for the distinction between all the frames actually recorded by an activation of the camera and the trimmed piece or pieces of that original group of frames which might be included in the worked text. Here Worth proposed "cademe" for the result of a single continuous activation of the camera and "edeme" for the frames which actually became part of the text. It must also be realized that while an edeme may be the smallest unit commonly physically manipulated in editing, it is not necessarily the case that object and depiction attributes are not considered at every point (i.e., every frame) during recording and editing-the term "use" must be considered carefully here.

An editor may choose to include the entire cademe, in which case it becomes an edeme. Generally, however, the edeme results when it is decided that the cademe as recorded is only partly acceptable (it is too long, something unwanted takes place during a portion of the recording time) or it is decided that the work's meaning would be stated more appropriately if pieces of the single recording were put together with pieces of other cademes. This leaves open the question of defining those portions of academe which are used at different locations throughout a text, especially if there was a change in the subject or the recording technique during the original recording session so that different portions of the same cademe have very different looks. Similarly, there is a problem in describing the results of the removal of some of the frames of a cademe with the implacement of no frames from some other cademe.

There is no bound on the actual or the relative number of frames to be contained within shot: cademe or edeme. The compounds of static objects, static camera, moving objects, and moving camera indicate that there is no bound on the content of a shot either. This lack of a bounded unit was a significant element in the move away from the linguistic model to describe film. Worth (1981) adopted a semiotic model for film communication because "it does not have units to which the same taxonomy of common significance can be applied as it can to verbal language."

Bonitzer (1977) notes that "shot'" seems to be "curiously free floating, badly defined, endlessly bifurcating into several meanings." This is not to say that the goal of a surrogate providing various levels of penetration is not within reason. Again, the notion of function as a major element of the definition of surrogate comes into play, as does Marr's notion that a representation highlights only some information. Some images together with some words and/or mathematical expressions may well be adequate to guide a user among many documents on similar topics. One might imagine at one level a few images together with a verbal statement such as "fast-paced editing and considerable close-up photography"; while at another level more images placed on a time line with expressions for the total number of image changes as a ratio of the work's running time; or even a more complex expression such as Watt's (1979) entropy measure of television programming attribute randomness. Other descriptive methods can be imagined and ought to be tested. Whether summaries of several structural aspects of a work are presented to a user or are deduced by the user from an information-rich secondary document, the maker of the surrogate and the user of the surrogate must realize that, while some questions might be answerable by the surrogate, it is intended only as a guide through the thickets of documents.

2.2.4   DISCUSSION

In order to determine what a surrogate should contain to provide this facility, consideration was given to the major differences in the relationship between a word and object and between a photographic image and object—the former being more or less arbitrary and conventional, the latter being more or less motivated or directly related to the object. The "more or less" is important, as even photographic images do not provide the same sort of perception1 stimulus set as do the objects themselves. Numerous variables can be manipulated to change the aspects of the object that are presented as significant. An important result of the difference between images and words is found in the combinations; that is, there cannot be said to be a specifiable syntax for moving image documents. The meaning of a moving image document (MID) is generated from a matrix of sequential phenomena. In order to provide a usable surrogate it was proposed that photographic images eliminate or alleviate problems found in the use of words to describe MIDs. Also, since structure is important to the generation of meaning but not easily partitioned or summarized by syntactic elements and generalizing terms, a matrix form was proposed as the means for presenting data about the moving image document. These are not necessarily new methods of conceiving the description of MIDs, rather they are, at least in part, the application of methods which have proven useful for the makers of MIDs now proposed as tools Many such questions remain to be asked and to be answered. In an age when technological advances are giving to users considerable ability to be actively involved with moving image texts we can examine more deeply examine the theoretical and practical means by which the book-like, personal scrutiny of these texts might be achieved.

Baudry (1980) addresses this point: "Perhaps when the conditions of film projection will change, through technical progresses which promise to allow us to have access at will to films, it may become possible to walk leisurely, to wander, to loaf about, stroll and loiter … delighted to explore the ordered depth of a film, to appreciate a thousand details in a sequence while experiencing the unique character of the whole."

2.3   STORY THREE: KEY FRAMES

At this point there was a substantial model of moving image documents and how they might be made more accessible; yet there was no mechanism for algorithmically extracting elements from a film document in any way similar to the automatic extraction of keywords that had been available for some decades. This was especially frustrating since, as a filmmaker, Brian had access to the equipment and working procedures. Film and video editors are the actual sculptors of structure. While the details vary, a common thread runs through much of the production practice. The time that an image appears and disappears from the screen, the precise point at which various sounds are heard, and the location of visual effects are all tied to a time line. Depending on the medium (video or film), the images are recorded in increments of 1/30th or 1/24th of a second. The document is essentially a strip of still images—24 or 30 for every second of running time. This provides an addressing mechanism that enables the precise measurement of structure necessary to map extra-topical attributes.

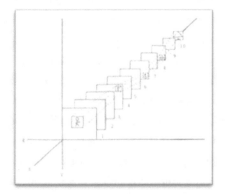

During the 1980s videodisc technology became available and enabled computer-controlled viewing of movies. We did a few experiments using access at the individual frame level and overlaying measurement software with the video. While this was only a partially automated approach and was cumbersome by today's standards, it did allow us to make progress on our modeling.

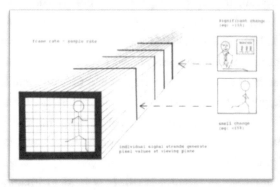

Figure 2.2: Early sketches of frame grid, three-dimensional model of film signal, and sampling data stream.

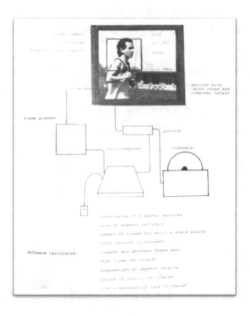

Representation of film texts for scholars and students has been fraught with difficulties imposed by the very nature of the text. The time-varying image track presented hurdles to close significant challenges to formulation of units of meaning and analysis. The digital environment offers opportunities for addressing these problems. We offer here a model of the film document as a bundle of time-varying signals. We demonstrate using this model to construct a system for close analysis of film texts, including precise measurement of attributes.

2.3.1   PROBLEM SETTING

Movies in a dark theater transport us to realms outside ourselves in a manner rather like the songs of Homer moved listeners along on a dream journey. Regardless of the mechanism, the appeal lies in being taken along at the pace and to the place dictated by the text. The technologies of writing and printing offer scholars an environment in which scholars might review and analyze a verbal text. Unfortunately, the scholar intent on close scrutiny of a film text has had few options but to make the dream journey several times—not infrequently with a flashlight between teeth and a notebook and pen in hand.

Mechanism has posed a major barrier to user control over locus of insertion, depth of penetration, and time of engagement. For decades, the film scholar sat in a dark room and watched the serial unrolling of the text. Sometimes this was in a theater where no control over the text was available; sometimes this was in a room with a projector that could be stopped, reversed, slowed, speeded up. In each case, however, the engagement required serial viewing; that is, all frames between any two points in the text had to be viewed. Even the scholar with access to film production equipment or later, videotape could not escape the serial nature of the engagement.

Reviewing *Caravagio's Secrets* (Bersani and Dutoit, 1998), a recent work on the baroque painter Michelangelo Caravaggio, Arthur Danto complained about the teaching of the history of art, congratulating the authors for *focusing our attention on the paintings themselves without lapsing into formalism* (Danto, 1998). It is hard to imagine the same comment being made about film studies where both formal analysis and the practice of what Danto calls *ekphrasis* (from the Greek for description: collaborative description that is sensitive to how meaning and pictorial detail are connected) have become a thing of the past. Why? Some reasons are theoretical and do not concern us here. Others are eminently practical and undermine the film scholars' best attempts to come to terms with the complex operations to produce the *film-effect*.

Videodisc technology enabled random access to points within a film text and a limited form restructuring the text. Yet two significant forms of intrusion of mechanism remained. The first resembled the long-standing problem of hardware—players need a separate computer (or digital gymnastics on a multi-button remote) and frequently two monitors. The second is fundamentally vexing—actually "grabbing" sections of a film text for comparison with others, or for comparison with words (e.g., a script or a journal article) required photographic copying of individual film frames with a still camera or, later, the use of a video printer. Even when this was accomplished one had only bundles of still pictures.

We can restate our motivation here as an attempt to come to grips with *the precarious balance between stillness and movement that we encounter at every step*. Ultimately, it is the transit from one still image to another which has defeated attempts to freeze the film-text as it turns into something else—a still photograph if you stop the machine, or any number of quasi-cinematic representations if you slow it down or speed it up. Yet it remains, in Bellour's term, *unattainable in motion* (Figure 2.3).

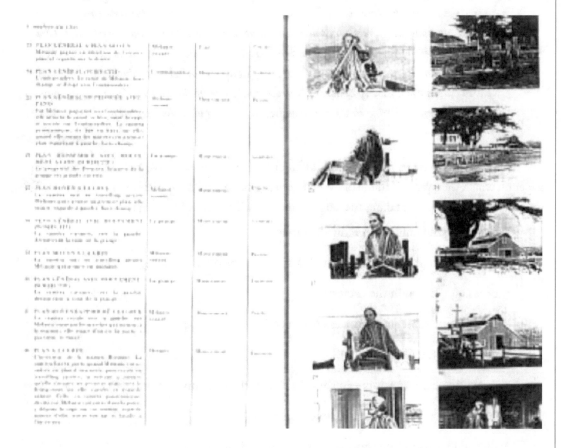

Figure 2.3: A Bellour text analyzing a segment of *The Birds*. There is no access to the motion component of the film, to the sound track, to the color. Frame enlargements are selected and produced manually.

The primary problem is the very nature of the moving image document; that is, the stillness/motion tango at the heart of the perceptual and technological mechanism. The shortcoming of most previous tools has been achievement of a small measure of control over the image text at the expense of the annihilation of the film effect. The urge to deal with the image/movement issue is what motivated this project. What the digital environment offers is precisely to have it both ways.

Thierry Kuntzel's close scrutiny of the effect produced by the defilement of a series of still images passing through the gates of a projector, and Raymond Bellour's analysis of the inflection of the film-text resulting from the director's intervention in the dialectics of the look in the diegesis of the film, and between the characters and the spectators, delineate a new space of investigation for film theory. Both studies deal with what is perhaps the most inaccessible, "unattainable" among the numerous operations which interact in the production of the cinema-effect, what Kuntzel also calls, "the filmic": that delicate balance between stillness and movement, whereby "the film-projection is generated by the film-strip in the denial of this same film-strip by the film-projection, in the rubbing out of the work of signification." A text which also is unattainable, in the sense first used by Bellour of "introuvable" by being literally and figuratively unquotable, everlastingly slipping through in the instance of being identified, seized for closer scrutiny .

Augst (1980a)

Over several decades we have used different tool environments. We have generated sheets of paper on which were printed frame blow-ups from segments of film, as pictured in Figure 1.1. These were made by a process of taking the original motion picture film in hand, then:

- eyeballing the film for an individual frame;

- setting the frame on registration pins in a copying device attached to a camera;

- exposing the film in the camera;

- locating any subsequent frames and repeating the process;

- developing the film;

- generating contact prints—images the size of the copy image frames;

- cutting those into individual frame prints;

- then gluing them into some order on a sheet of paper; and

- duplicating the sheet of paper.

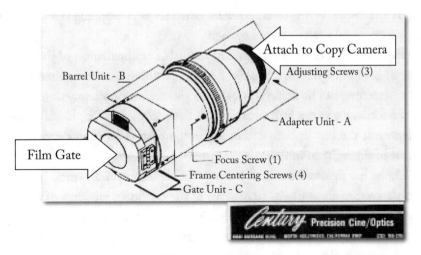

Figure 2.4: Instructions for the Century Duplikin Device for Copying Individual Film Frames.

This was, to say the least, time consuming. In addition, the small size of the images together with the similarity of any one frame in a sequence to the next led to frequent confusions.

See Figure 2.5 for a model of the filmic representation mechanism. If we were to:

- set up a movie camera at a rodeo;

- begin recording shortly before the arrival of a horse and rider;

- leave the camera running as the horse and rider go by; and

- stop recording when the rider has fallen off,

then we would have a representation that would play back the colors and shapes of the horse and rider in the same sequence and for the same duration as in the original event. Such a representation depends on sampling a data stream at a given interval and frequency, then playing back the sampled data at the same interval and frequency. If Homer had had a video camera, there would be little puzzling over just how the "wine dark sea" looked or just what a "well-greaved Achaean" carried for weaponry (though the issue of Athena's appearance might be more problematic.)

Yet, the Homeric story and the film text depend on more than mere playback of single event data streams. Compression, expansion, substitution, and weaving together of different story strands are the stuff of story telling. Accomplishing these with an understanding of an audience's coding system distinguishes reportage from the engaging tale. The pre-Homeric scholar attempting to do a structural analysis of a heroic tale would have been in a difficult position. Engagement with the text would have meant going to a performance, listening for words or metrical patterns that recurred, and … what? Perhaps remember those words or patterns, then go to a second performance and pick up a stone for each occurrence. With several graduate assistants each dropping stones for a different attribute, perhaps a structural analysis would emerge.

The post-Homeric scholar has access to a manipulable representation of the story—words printed on paper or held in digital files. Words and their positions can be counted or graphed; a segment near the beginning can be copied (or cut out) and set beside a segment near the end for comparison; patterns in one text can be compared with those in another. The digital post-Homeric scholar can re-represent the text in binary form and accomplish word counts and frequencies or statistical measures of similarity in minutes

The film scholar has followed a similar journey. The digital environment for moving images is now sufficiently robust to allow digital translation of the enormous amounts of data in a video segment. We can now return time to the representation palette. We can now bring book-like ca-pabilities to film scholarship. We can, with some thought, humility, and insight step beyond the book-like engagement with film and put different forms of evidence onto the same platform.

2.3.2   UNITS OF MEANING

The digital environment enables the film theorist, the film producer, and the film student to make use of a more rigorous and more widely applicable vocabulary of analysis. The difficulties in repre-senting moving image documents lie, in part, in the literary metaphor. There is not in the moving image document a sequence of minimal units of meaning subject to easy demarcation. Where the physical verbal print document is a single ordered set of discrete and definable units (i.e., letters or phonemes), the physical moving image document is comprised of multiple strands of data—light values at different points on a plane surface, often together with multiple levels of sound.

Word-based descriptors of units of meaning as well as stylistic categories are of little help. Terms such as shot, close up (CU) medium shot (MS), long shot (LS), and documentary, which are common in film theory and in cataloging rules, lack precise definitions, are "endlessly bifur-cated" (Bonitzer, 1977) and, thus, severely limit the powers for discrimination and analysis. Is a CU anything that occupies more than 50% of the image area? 60%? 80%? Genre terms such as "documentary" say very little about what to expect of a work's content or structural characteristics.

How might we use the time line concept common to producers to construct precise and gen-eralizable processes for abstracting moving image documents? How might we enhance the recogni-tion and understanding … attendant upon structural consideration, so as to enable discrimination within and among works on similar topics? While the utility of structural representations has long been recognized by producers and artists, so have the limitations of structure charts developed for personal use without replicable and transportable units and modes of representation. That is, charts of structural relations have been used frequently by film and video producers, but they have been based on the production requirements and the working habits of the production crew. The elements are not standardized and often deal with minutiae beyond the representation needs of most users. Still, their long-term use in the field suggests that they yield a robust model for representation. The three-dimensional model uses a timeline element in the form of one of the three axes.

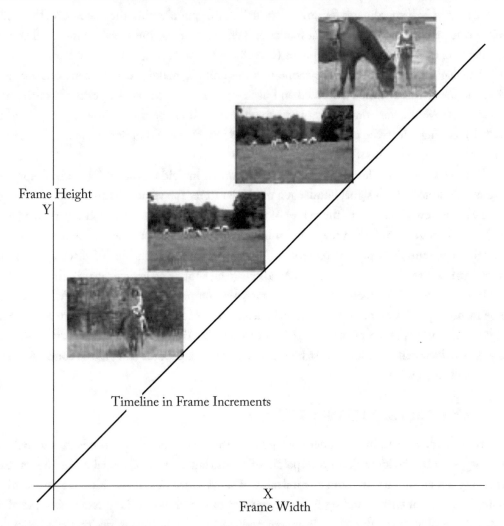

Figure 2.5: Three-dimensional, time-varying, pixel-based model of film text.

Visualizing a timeline with each of the frames stacked along it presented a stream of data, as illustrated in Figure 2.5. Modeling the moving image document as a bundle or stream of stimulus values means that one can apply procedures for the measurement of signal variability.

The signal bundle model assumes a virtual, continuous signal or cluster of signals—strands in a bundle—in depth. Each moving image document frame is a perpendicular slice across the signal bundle. The frame transects the signal bundle and reveals a matrix of strand values. The frame sets the vertical and horizontal bounds of the matrix; the cells of the matrix are pixels (picture elements).

The frame is the constant, regular, and addressable unit of measure within a (MID). It is a sampling mechanism which provides a reference point within the length of the document and it provides a set of X,Y coordinates for any individual sample point within the document. This makes possible comparisons within individual frames and among frames. The Z-axis is the third component, allowing measurements across frames (essentially, time). It should be noted here that in the days of analog filmmaking, while the frame was the unit for making editing decisions, elements within the frame could still be discussed and used—making the cut at the point where the hand reaches just above the horizon; waiting until about one third of the frame showed the pink of the sunset sky; cutting where the movement of the horses foot at the end of one sequence just matches the location and movement of the seagull in the next.

The pixel is the smallest addressable unit within an individual frame. Each pixel represents the value of a strand of the signal bundle at a particular time. The value of each strand of the signal bundle can be viewed relative to the values of all other strands in the bundle at a particular plane (time), as well as to the values in the same strand and other strands at other frame planes.

The representations present patterns of changes in the relationships of pixel values, rather than extractions based on mechanical demarcations (e.g., shot or cademe or word). Each pixel can be addressed with X, Y, Z coordinates. Precise analysis, comparison, and display of MID elements can be made by precise numeric and formulaic description of location (X, Y) and extent (Z). Such an approach removes much of the ambiguity of earlier descriptive terminology. It also allows for tracking one document attribute across boundaries of other attributes (e.g., music continuing even when a "shot" has ended).

2.3.3   ANALYSIS ENVIRONMENT

Extraction of key frames, in a manner analogous to the extraction of key words in a verbal text, is accomplished by the identification of points of significant change of spatial and temporal data. This is very similar to the way automatic indexing of word-based documents identifies keywords by looking for points of change and significant frequency of occurrence. This system makes use of the numerical precision of the digital environment and the processing capabilities that can be applied to the numerical data to measure temporal aspects, size of an object or portion of an image, and the coordinates of an image segment within the field.

During the extraction process, the program tools are superimposed over the images being analyzed. The software tracks attributes of user-identified objects:

- point at which object appears,

- size,

- location on screen,

- position relative to other objects,

- duration on screen, and

- movement on screen.

Points of significant change are noted; the degree of change considered significant is user selectable.

2.3.4   DOCUMENT DISCRIMINATION

As an early experiment to test such an approach to analysis, we attempted to discriminate between two moving image documents on the same topic—women running the marathon. In several informal screenings of the two documents, we gathered viewer opinions of the two videos. Document A was almost always described as *dynamic, exciting, engaging, emotional*; Document B was almost always described as *dull, boring, snoozer*. Yet, both documents showed approximately 50 women running 26 miles in urban settings.

+ 50 women running in urban setting

+ Derive for each frame
    + Pixels/frame occupied by each woman
    + Location in frame

+ Calculate
    + Percentage of size change
    + Percentage of location change
    Mean on-screen time
    + LA   4.99 seconds
    + Moscow 14.98 seconds
    Mean difference in areas
    + LA   55767 pixels
    + Moscow 28394 pixels.

+ Coach admonition: depends on audience

Each and every frame (1/30th second) of the two marathon documents was observed on the computer monitor and measurements were entered directly into the program. The software calculated values for several variables at each frame and then made comparisons across frames. This frame by frame analysis of the two marathon documents does make apparent significant differences in structure, and gives a precise representation of what might cause the term *dull* to be applied to one document and not the other.

The test system marked each point in each document where the area occupied by the primary object changed by 15% or more; and each change in object (e.g., head and shoulders image of Joan Benoit in one frame, then body of Grete Weitz in the next frame). The frames between any marked point of change and the succeeding marked point of change are termed an image set. The threshold for % object area change is variable from 0–100% within the test environment. The discrimination test used 15% as a small but significant number for the pattern recognition capabilities of the human visual system. A figure much lower than this is easily discerned, but it will likely present changes which result merely from minor (difference that doesn't make a difference) motions by the objects or from camera motion unavoidable in documentary recording. For example, in the marathon videos, the camera was often on a motorcycle alongside the runners; potholes in the road would cause minor variations in the camera/object relationship.

2.3.5   RESULTS

The salient figures from the analyses of the two marathon videos showed 3:1 ratios of longest image set lengths, range, and mean lengths, indicating very different structures. While Document A is only 58% as long as Document B, it is made up of 174% as many image sets. In a similar manner, the runners in Document A typically occupy nearly twice (196%) the screen area of those in Document B. In the current data Object 2 represents the average area of an individual runner within a recorded group of runners. The near 2:1 ratio holds throughout the documents.

Some 90% of Document A image sets lie within the 10-second range, with a rapid decline to the single longest image at 19 seconds (17–20). Document B, on the other hand, presents a less dramatic rise and fall and has nearly 30% of its image sets in a length range where Document A has none at all. This means that in Document A we are presented with faster paced editing (more image sets of shorter length) and that the women pictured are larger on the screen.

There is no value judgment implicit in the data yielded by the analysis of the two videos. Even if the hypothesis that rapid visual processing is more enjoyable, all else being equal, we must remember that all else is often not equal. The contour map indicating rapid change in data does not say: *This is better.* The contour map indicating slower pace does not state: *This is dull.* A topographic map of hill terrain does not make an evaluation of hill compared to plains. A weather map with closely spaced isobars does not say: *Windy weather is better.* A running coach who viewed the two documents pointed out that if he wanted parents to be excited enough to donate money to buy new uniforms, he would show Document A; yet if he wanted to show his runners how to strategize and how to "read" the other runners in a race, he would show Document B.

2.3.6   KEY FRAMES AND STRUCTURE PATTERNS

Tracking continuities of attributes and seeking points of discontinuity provides a means of representing document structure, and, thus, the foundational material for abstracts. Frames on either side of a point of discontinuity are key frames. Key frames and structural attributes are the principal entities used to reveal something essential about a moving image document. They are smaller quantities which make available the virtue and power of the document in a medium-specific manner. They are the boundaries of differences that make a difference. The data entered into the test environment program for any particular document can be used for numerous sorts of analysis and access. Individual frames, sets of frames, and alphanumeric and graphical data derived directly from the frames are used to construct a variety of abstracts.

This early computational analysis of the two marathon videos demonstrates the possibilities of machine-augmented determination of structural attributes and key image frames in a manner capable of providing adequate power for discrimination and analysis. Presenting the points of discontinuity to users is analogous to a topographic map. Various attributes at varying levels of detail are made evident. The idiosyncrasies of extraction, evaluation, and verbal tagging are left largely to the user.

The attributes described here are by no means the only attributes of moving image documents that might be of interest to users, nor are they the only attributes subject to precise description in a manner similar to that used here. Other attributes such as color values and luminance may not only be of interest but may also provide the means for more fully automated structure analysis. The audio tracks that accompany some moving image documents also present challenges and opportunities. In all these cases the numeric and formulaic processes for tracking discontinuities would remain the same.

Deriving the virtue and power from moving image documents is significantly enhanced by the application of digital technology and the modeling it allows. The precise description and addressing enable book-like access. Linking user navigation through the document to data about its structure enables user participation in sampling and meaning construction analogous to those customary in print documents with abstracts, indexes, and forms of marking such as post-it notes and bending corners. In a way, constructing document contour maps is analogous to an automatic indexing program for print verbal documents, but because of the complexity of visual documents, their image based nature, and the potential of the digital environment, contour maps are able to produce a variety of rich representations which:

- are based on the physically present text;

- involve the user to some degree;

- do not affix concept tags; and

- present different sorts of image based abstracts.

Contour maps enable navigation in ways familiar from the use of print documents, as well as ways familiar from navigating physical space. The benefits of pre-constructed representations and idiosyncratic exploration can be combined into a single system.

2.3.7   PEDAGOGICAL ENVIRONMENT

To return to the title of our piece: the digital environment means theorists and students now have means to come to grips with the *precarious balance between stillness and movement that we encounter at every step*. We can speak closely and carefully about production elements in a way that others will understand. We have the means for quantifying and making use of elements across time—describing and making use of discontinuities.

Even in the digital environment, the moving image text remains, to some degree, unattainable in motion. The book provides an analog for this situation—reading the print text of Homer's Iliad, is not and cannot be the same as hearing the poet recite the work; yet it proves to be a reasonable means of engaging the information, as well as giving it close scrutiny.

Of course, there are cautions to be given. We agree most whole-heartedly with Arrowsmith (1969) when he says:

> *I know of no art with such potential for stating our problems, complexities, anxieties, and powers more naturally or comprehensively than film. Yet we recognize the inherent dangers in analysis, the dangers of lapsing into formalisms to which Danto alludes, the dangers of castrating art, by disguising its true subversiveness, or by forcing it to yield a crop of acceptable clichés.*

A robust environment for explaining the mechanisms of film and for examining the complexities of its structure may enable the ekphraksis, the meaningful and engaged description that heightens the utility of film texts. Availability of the native elements of the original document in their original temporal sequence, together with a variety of tools for learning of others thoughts while generating one's own descriptions are at the heart of our stream bundle model and our experimental CD-ROM environment.

2.4   STORY FOUR: FUNCTIONAL ONTOLOGY

> *The functional ontology is the set of environmental stimuli and historic factors that have function for and individual at a particular point in time—those things that select behavior.*
>
> Rich Anderson (2006)

We began working together on modeling filmic structure in the early days of the new century. The notion of functional ontology proved to be the catalyst a robust model and tool set for analyzing, describing, and working with video documents.

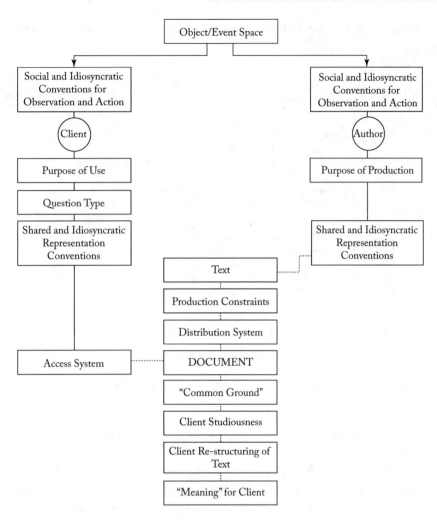

Figure 2.6: Earlier "common ground" model.

Blending Patrick Wilson's "turn to the functional" with the behaviorist notion of "anteced-ents, behavior, consequence" yielded a significantly more robust foundation for modeling filmic structure. Early on, we had modeled the relationship between a message maker and a seeker, high-lighting the similarities between the two actors and yielding a version of a "common ground" model. While this spoke to the constraints on coding by the message maker and constraints on decoding (thus on "meaning) for the seeker, applying radical behaviorist notions to the model removed the possible hint of sequentiality and overt parallelism from the early model. The functional ontology model loosens up any implied notions of parallel time or abilities or circumstance between the message maker and the seeker. At the same time it provides a means for developing a useful line of experimenting, as noted below in our description of computational modeling based on human expert behavior.

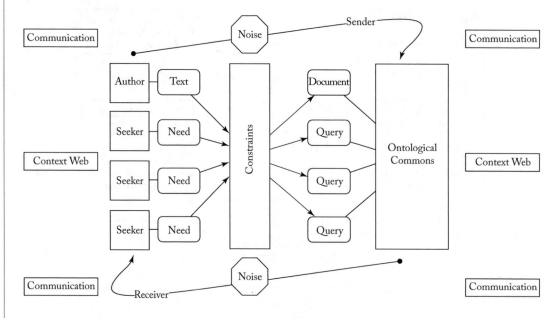

Figure 2.7: Antecedents, behaviors, and consequences—functional ontology model.

2.4.1   LOOKING TO THE PRACTICE OF FILM EDITING

We developed one more model to engage our thinking about Bellour, *The Birds*, and filmic structure—an instantiation of traditional film editor practice. Before video films were edited by hand and eye, sometimes with the aid of a magnifying mechanism and motorized movement at "film speed." One common practice was to hang strips of film on small pins with a bright wall or light box behind so that the individual frames were visible. The editor would have seen the film projected beforehand, so that just a hint of the look was usually sufficient for making a selection from the film bin.

We took the basic idea of strips of film and applied it to the more than 12,000 frames of the sequence of film we were planning to examine—the Bodega Bay sequence of *The Birds* that Raymond Bellour had analyzed. We printed all the frames at near actual size onto a single five-foot by eight-foot sheet of photographic paper. While the frames were printed in horizontal strips rather than the vertical orientation of the editor's film bin, the result was quite similar. One can already make out the basics of the structure identified by Bellour (1969) without even knowing either the film as a whole or what is shown in each of the individual frames.

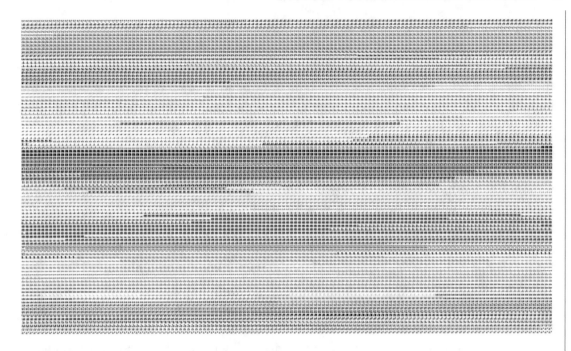

Figure 2.8: More than 12,000 frames from the Bodega Bay sequence of *The Birds*.

2.4.2   AUTOMATING THE SEMIOTIC ANALYSIS OF FILM

In 1981, film theorist Bertrand Augst asked in a conversation, "Why can't we use a computer to measure and speak of filmic structure in the same way we can for verbal text?" Augst's question arose in a conversation on the difficulties for film studies that arise from the "literary metaphor." This is not to say there is no discourse mechanism at work in films; it is that attempts at one-to-one correspondence between the frame and the word or the shot and the sentence or similar impositions of the verbal form onto the image form failed. Films are not textual documents. Films do not have a rigidly defined grammatical structure. Images are not words. Pryluck (1976) asserts that shots are not sentences. Films are generally viewed at a set rate of presentation and linearity. The technology used in the production and viewing of film has changed considerably since Augst (Augst and O'Connor, 1999) posed his original question; however, there has been little change or advancement in film theory as a result of better and more efficient technology.

2.4.3   THE STRUCTURE OF MOVING IMAGE DOCUMENTS

It has been common in both film description and film analysis to use the "shot" as the base or minimum unit. However, there is no definition of shot that specifies any specific set of parameters for any particular attribute—no specific number of frames or type of content. Bonitzer (1977) refers to definitions of *shot* as "endlessly bifurcated." Similarly, the terms *close up* (CU), *medium shot* (MS), and *long shot* (LS) are used in film production textbooks and film analyses; however, there is no specification of how much frame real estate is occupied by some object or portion of object in the frame to be a CU rather than MS, for example. We use the frame and measurable attributes of the frame to speak specifically and to avoid the difficulties presented by "endless bifurcation."

The signal or the information of a film is presented in small units—frames—that are in themselves self-contained signals. In many instances they are even used as messages (e.g., an individual frame may become a movie poster). However, the film and other time-varying signal sets such as music and dance are signal sets of their given sort precisely because of their temporality. We see or hear the signal set (document) as a set of changes over time.

One could stare at a painting or sculpture for an hour from differing viewpoints, thus making the viewing a time-varying experience of the signal set. It could probably be argued that artists of various sorts construct signal sets that demand attention for a long time in order to see all the intended variations in the signal set. It can even be argued (and we have so argued) that the digital environment gives viewers reader-like control over temporality and depth of penetration into films.

However, it remains the case that the majority of film produced for commercial consumption assumes playback at a standard rate and linearity. Much of what is taught in film schools and much of what has transpired in film analysis relates to variation in the temporal aspect of the film. Eisenstein (1969) and Vertov (1984) and some others spoke eloquently of time and its relation to structure. Structural commentary from reviewers tends to be less precise. For example, LaSalle (2005) describes *The Legend of Zorro* as a "130-minute adventure movie that overstays its welcome by about 80 minutes," and Addiego (2005) describes *Domino* as "[a] psychedelic action picture that hammers away at the audience with a barrage of editing tics and tricks."

We are seeking a way to speak of the structure of a film precisely in order to enable a more productive examination of the meanings of the message for various viewers under various circumstances. In looking to previous work on the examination of the filmic message or signal set, we noted Augst's (1980b) comment on Bellour's (1969) analysis of Hitchcock's (2000) *The Birds*: "It remains exemplary in the rigor and precision of the analysis performed and, to date, it is still the best example of what a genuine structural analysis of a filmic text could attempt to do. One must turn to Jakobson or Ruwet to find anything comparable in literary studies."

A comment by Augst (1980b) on Bellour's response to criticism of his work as pseudo-scientific and not sufficiently in touch with aesthetic aspects of film analysis addressed our particular concerns with devising an accurate and transferable means of describing the signal set: "[criticisms] continue to be leveled at any procedure that in any way exposes the gratuitousness and arbitrariness of impressionistic criticism."

Bellour's work elaborated on Metz's (1974) semiotic notions of film, particularly the concept of syntagmas, by introducing levels of segmentation greater and lesser than Metz's. This enabled structural analysis of filmic signal sets of any length and, eventually, of any sort, not simply the set, say, of classic American Hollywood features.

2.4.4   DIFFICULTIES FOR BELLOUR

We identified two difficulties with Bellour's signal set analysis. The first was the time-consuming nature of its practice. Simply locating the proper portions of film, timing them, re-photographing frames for analysis and publication, to say nothing of commentary or analysis, took days and weeks.

The second is that Bellour conducted his work too early—for the remarkable precision of Bellour's analysis, without digital technology he did not have a precise system of description at the frame level. He could write of contents of the frame and of relationships holding among frames, but not with deep precision (e.g., the shades of various colors and their changes from frame to frame).

The digital environment enables us to address both issues. Grabbing all the individual frames from a digital version of a film requires only seconds, not days. Also, pixels enable addressable analysis of the red, green, blue, and luminance components of any point in the frame, as well as comparisons of values at the same point or set of points across time. The mechanics of the practice of film analysis, which once would have required enormous resources of time, funding and technology are today essentially trivial.

However, the technical ability to address and measure points within and across frames does not address Augst's earlier question; nor does it, in itself, provide a "genuine structural analysis of filmic texts." We have the technology—but what should we do with it? Techniques for analyzing the structure of moving image documents are well known and mature. Dailianas, Allen, and England (1995) reviewed a number of techniques for the segmentation of video including techniques for measuring the absolute difference between successive frames, several histogram-based methods, as well as the measurement of objects within frames. These techniques proved to be robust when compared against human observers; however, all techniques were prone to false positives. They note that: "[b]ecause all the methods studied here have high false-identification rates, they should be thought of as providing suggestions to human observers and not as an ultimate standard of performance."

Structure and function have a complementary, but independent relationship. In order to advance the state of both structural and theoretical analysis, the relationship between structure and function must be taken into account. In other words, an analysis that takes both structure and function into account is greater than the sum of its parts. Kearns and O'Connor (2004) provide a strong example of this approach in their demonstration of the relationship between the entropic structure of television programs and the preferences of a group of viewers.

The approach taken here combines an algorithmic structural analysis of the Bodega Bay sequence of Hitchcock's *The Birds* with the expert analysis of Bellour. Our hope is that a heuristic will emerge that will lead toward a solution to the problems identified both by film theorists and those who wish to analyze moving image documents for the purposes of indexing and retrieval.

2.4.5   BINARY SYSTEMS OF STRUCTURE AND FUNCTION

We are using the technical definition posited by Claude Shannon and we state strongly our support of Warren Weaver's comment in his introduction to Shannon's *Mathematical Theory of Communication* (1949):

> *The word* information, *in this theory, is used in a special sense that must not be confused with its ordinary usage. In particular information must not be confused with meaning. [p. 8] The concept of information developed in this theory at first seems disappointing and bizarre—disappointing because it has nothing to do with meaning, and bizarre because it deals not with a single message but rather with the statistical character of a whole ensemble of messages, bizarre also because in these statistical terms the two words* information *and* uncertainty *find themselves to be partners.*

However, it is the very distinction between information and meaning that provides a theory base and descriptive tool-kit for the description and analysis of film. For Shannon, information is the amount of freedom of choice in the construction of a message. This concept was ordinarily expressed as a logarithmic function of the number of choices. What is important is Shannon's assertion that the semantic aspects of communication have no relevance to the engineering aspects; however, the engineering aspects are not necessarily irrelevant to the semantic aspects.

Shannon's notion of information is a binary system. Message and meaning are separate, but complementary notions. This system bears a strong resemblance to the distinction between signifier and signified in semiotic theory, as well as the separation of topography and function in the behavior analytic theory of verbal behavior as outlined by Skinner (1957) and Catania, (1998) and Wittgenstein's notion of a language game as in Wittgenstein (1953) and Day and Leigland (1992).

Our model for analysis assumes such a binary relationship. The structural analysis was conducted by measuring the changes in color palette across frames in the Bodega Bay sequence of Hitchcock's *The Birds*. The functional analysis comes from Bellour's analysis of the same sequence of the film.

2.4.6   FUNCTIONAL ANALYSIS "SYSTEM OF A FRAGMENT" (BELLOUR)

Behavior analysis is an empirical and functional way to examine questions involving human behavior. Skinner (1957) describes the logic of a functional analysis:

The external variables of which behavior is a function provide for what may be called a causal or functional analysis. We undertake to predict and control the behavior of an individual organism. This is our "dependent variable"—the effect for which we are to find the cause. Our "independent variables"—the causes of behavior—are the external conditions of which behavior is a function. Relations between the two—the "cause-and-effect relationships" in behavior are the laws of a science. A synthesis of these laws expressed in quantitative terms yields a comprehensive picture of the organism as a behaving system.

Why is this logic important to our seeking a conceptual framework and set of tools for structural analysis of film? Our question concerns the relationship between the physical structure of the Bodega Bay sequence of *The Birds* and Bellour's description of the structure of the sequence. In other words, what physical attributes of the sequence prompted Bellour to make the statements he made about the film?

The notion of a binary system is so fundamental that we need to re-make an earlier statement: a behavior analytic account of verbal behavior is a binary system. The structure or topography of a particular instance of verbal behavior has a complementary, but separate, relationship with the function or meaning of that particular instance. The behavior analytic account is similar in many respects to the separation of message and meaning in Shannon's work as well as semiotic theories of meaning. Behavior analysis provides an analytical language and framework that is appropriate for the problem at hand.

Catania (1998) defines a *tact* as "a verbal response occasioned by a discriminative stimulus." A discriminative stimulus is a stimulus that occasions a particular response and is correlated with reinforcement. In this particular case, the tacts or verbal responses of interest are the statements about the Bodega Bay sequence made by Bellour and Penly (2002) in *The Analysis of Film*. The discriminative stimuli are the physical dimensions of the film that prompted Bellour to make the statements he did in *The Analysis of Film*. The reinforcement in this case is assumed on the grounds that The Analysis of Film is considered to be a seminal work in the film theory community and Bellour and others applied the same types of analysis to other films.

2.4.7   FUNCTIONAL ANALYSIS OF BELLOUR'S VERBAL BEHAVIOR

We sought a means of structural analysis in turning to the expertise of Raymond Bellour. We selected a piece of his rigorous analysis, "System of a Fragment: On *The Birds*" (originally "les Oiseaux: analyse d'une séquence" (Bellour, 1969); using it as a record of his engagement with the signal set of a portion of the Hitchcock film. We captured the frames from the sequence for a data set of 12,803 frames. We then decided to determine how much of Bellour's response could be accounted for by one element of the data—the distribution of color across each and every frame. That is, we did not account for sound, for edge detection or for previous knowledge.

The sequence is, on the surface, rather simple. A young woman, Melanie Daniels, sets out in a small motorboat with a pair of lovebirds in a cage. She crosses Bodega Bay to leave the birds as a gift to catch the attention of a young man, Mitch Brenner. She enters the Brenner's house, leaves the birds, and returns to the boat to go back across the bay. Mitch spots Melanie crossing the bay. Mitch drives around the bay to the pier where Melanie will be arriving. A sea gull strikes Melanie and cuts her head before she reaches the pier. Mitch helps Melanie out of the boat and they walk toward a shop to tend to the wound.

When Melanie is on the bay, Bellour points out, we are presented with a classic Hollywood form, alternation—we see on the screen Melanie looking, then that at which she looks, then Melanie again. This form continues until she arrives at the house. While she is in the house we simply observe her behavior, except for a brief look out the window at the barn. Bellour sees this scene in the house as a "hinge" in the design of the film. It disrupts the pattern of alternation, while it also takes Melanie off the water.

As Melanie returns to the boat, we see what looks rather like the beginning of her trip—she is getting into the boat and heading off. However, Mitch sees her; then she and Mitch acknowledge one another. Bellour refers to the scene in the house (the hinge) and the double act of seeing as the "two centers" of the Bodega Bay sequence.

As an integral portion of his analytic writing, Bellour includes photographic frames from the Bodega Bay sequence—key frames. Ordinarily, these are the first frames of each shot in the sequence. However, this is not always the case. The difficulties of defining "shots" seem to be manifested here. We will discuss this point at greater length; for now, "shot" is ordinarily understood to be a mechanical unit—all the frames from camera original film (or a working copy) left in by an editor. Thus, all the beginning frames, where the camera comes up to speed, the director shouts, "action" and the miscues before usable footage is available, are cut out. Then a set of frames—each a still image representing approximately 1/30th of a second—shows the portion of the action desired by the director. Then a cut—in film, an actual mechanical cut; in video, still a cessation of a particular stream of data—is made and another shot appended. The process is repeated until the end of the film.

Ordinarily, especially in older films, there is a close correlation between the mechanical cuts and the data within the shot. However, there is a problem here for the definition of *shot*—data may change even in one run of the camera or one stream of frames between cuts. The camera may remain still while various objects come and go in front of it; the camera may move and present different views of the same objects or even different objects; the camera may remain still, but have the length of its lens changed during a shot; or various combinations of these may take place. For the viewer, whether several objects or views are shown in different shots or one shot may be of little overt consequence. However, in attempting do critical analysis, one is faced with finding a unit of meaning or, at least, a unit of address and measure that provides precision of description.

In our analysis, we operate at the level of the individual frame (29.97 frames per second.) We refer to Bellour's shot numbers and to his two primary divisions: "A" for Melanie's trip across the bay, her time in the house and her return to the boat; "B" for her return trip in the boat.

According to Bellour's analysis and textual description of the Bodega Bay sequence, then we should expect to find the following tacts (verbal responses to the film) in the physical document: key frames and key frame sets, alternation, two centers—the "hinge" sequence and a second center.

In summary, Bellour identified the following features in the physical document: key frames and key frame sets, alternation, two centers—the "hinge" sequence and a second center when Melanie and Mitch see each other. The question is: Can we identify elements in the physical structure of the film that could have stimulated his verbal responses (tacts)?

2.4.8   STRUCTURAL ANALYSIS OF THE BODEGA BAY SEQUENCE

There are several approaches that could be applied to the structural analysis of a film. Salt (2003) advocates an approach based on the notion of the "shot" and the statistical character and distribution of "shots" within a moving image document. O'Connor (1991) and Kearns and O'Connor (2004) employed an information theoretic approach to the analysis of film. O'Connor (1991) used a technique that measured the change of the size and position of objects or, more accurately, pixel clusters within a film. Dailianas, Allen, and England (1995) reviewed a number of automated techniques for the automatic segmentation of films that included the analysis of raw image differences between frames, a number of histogram-based techniques and an edge detection-based approach.

In choosing a technique for structural analysis of a film, the nature of the question one hopes to answer must be taken into account. An information theory approach such as that taken by Kearns and O'Connor (2004) measures the structure of an entire film or message in Shannon and Weaver's (1949) terms. Bellour described the Bodega Bay sequence in fairly microscopic detail. An information theoretic approach would not be granular enough to adequately match Bellour's description. It should be noted that Kearns' concept of "entropic bursts"(2005) might provide a finer grained information theoretic appropriate for the task at hand. Salt's (2003) statistical approach based on the analysis of shots is limited in a number of respects. The previously discussed conceptual problems with the "shot" as a unit of analysis make Salt's approach untenable. In addition, Salt's analysis examines the statistical character and description of shots over the course of a complete film or collection of moving image documents. Like the information theoretic approach, Salt's approach is macroscopic. Finally, the phenomena addressed by Salt's methods are not congruent with elements of the moving image document that Bellour addresses in his analysis. The segmentation techniques reviewed by Dailianas, Allen, and England (1995) provide the level of detail necessary for the detection of key frames and frame sets in Bellour's analysis; however, they would not be appropriate for detecting alternation or detecting the centers within the sequence as identified by Bellour.

Our ultimate goal in analyzing the structure of the Bodega Bay sequence was to find the elements of the physical structure of the moving image document that prompted Bellour to make the statements (tacts) he did about the film. To accomplish this task, it was necessary to look at the structure of the segment on at least two levels. First, Bellour breaks the sequence into "shots" or frame sets and selects key frames. This requires an examination of individual frames. Second, Bellour describes alternation between the frame sets, the unique character of the "hinge," the two centers and the gull strike. These tacts are descriptions of the relationship between frame sets.

We sought precise, repeatable, numeric, and graphical representations of the signal that would enable discussion of filmic structure—the message, in the terms of Shannon and Weaver. We sought the means by which we might discuss message structure, so that discussions of meaning would have a significant touchstone. It might be said that we sought a method of fingerprinting the frames.

In standard digital images each and every color is composed of a certain amount of red, a certain amount of green and a certain amount of blue—with black being the absence of any red, green or blue and with white being maximum of each. In the frame images we captured there is a possibility of 256 shades of red, 256 shades of green, and 256 shades of blue for a possible palette of over 16 million colors. Deriving a histogram of each of the RGB components or the aggregated values distributed across an X-axis of 255 points (the zero origin being the 256th) yields a fingerprint—a color distribution map—of each frame.

Perhaps one of the most appealing aspects of mapping color distribution is that it is an entirely software-based process. There is no necessity for human intervention to determine and mark what is to be considered the "subject" or how many pixels (what percentage of the frame area) make up some viewer-selected object. Not that these are not useful for some sorts of analysis, but using just the color palette enables an essentially judgment-free analytic process.

2.4.9   METHOD OF PIXEL-LEVEL ANALYSIS

Structural Analysis. We converted the Bodega Bay to an AVI file and then extracted the individual frames to 12,803 JPG image files. We generated RGB histograms for each of the 12,803 frames using the Python Imaging Library. A Lorenz transformation was then performed on each histogram. We calculated a Gini coefficient for each frame to generate a scalar value representing the color distribution of each frame. The Gini coefficient compares a perfectly even distribution of RGB against the actual distribution in each frame. We used the differences in Gini coefficients between successive frames as a measure of change across frames.

Codifying Bellour's Analysis. Bellour's analysis does not include precise times or frame numbers to either select key frames or delineate frame sets; however, he includes photographs of the key frames. The frame numbers for Bellour's key frames and frame set boundaries were selected using visual comparison between the photographs from Bellour's article and the extracted frames. Frame sets were composed of all the frames between successively identified key frames and tagged using Bellour's numbering convention. Bellour grouped frame sets into higher-level groups. The frame sets were arranged into higher level groups using Bellour's description.

2.4.10 RESULTS

Due to the differences in precision between Bellour's analysis and the structural analysis, we believed that visual analysis would be the most appropriate option for the task at hand. Bellour's analysis began with shot number 3 of the segment and continued to shot 84. Bellour includes two groups of shots that have little bearing on his analysis of the sequence: Melanie's acquisition and boarding of the boat (3–12) and Melanie's arrival at the dock following her trip and the gull strike (84a–84f). These sets do not play into Bellour's analysis and appear to function only to demarcate the segment within the larger document—the entire film of *The Birds*.

Detection of key frames and frame sets. Figure 2.9 shows the absolute value of the difference between the Gini value of a particular frame of the Bodega Bay sequence of The Birds and the previous frame. The mean difference between frames for all frames in the sequence is 0.003826, which is represented on the graph by the green (lower) horizontal line. The mean difference between frames identified as key frames by Bellour was 0.075678. The difference values fall into a bimodal distribution. The difference values of key frames and the proceeding frame were an order of magnitude higher than the difference values between frames that were not identified as key frames. Figure 2.10 shows the Gini coefficients for each frame broken down into individual frame sets as identified by Bellour. Within shots, the Gini coefficients remain stable for most shots and trend in a linear manner. Notable exceptions to this pattern include the group of frame sets that make up Bellour's "hinge" sequence (25–43); the gull strike (77); and Melanie's arrival at the dock following the gull strike (84a–84f).

Analysis of frame sets. Figure 2.10 shows the Gini coefficients of each frame of the segment broken down by shot number, presenting the flow of the color distributions across the time of the film sequence. We might construct a tact map by over-layering indicators for some of the key elements mapped by the data in Figure 2.10, as in Figure 2.11. Once Melanie is actually underway on her trip to the Brenner house, we have almost uninterrupted alternation. We are presented with Melanie in the boat, then the Brenner house as she sees it—Bellour's shots 15–22. Then we are presented with Melanie paddling the boat and seeing the dock—23–24; then walking on the dock and seeing the barn—25–31. That is, shots 15–31 present Melanie, what she sees, Melanie, what she sees, and so on. The latter portion is more distinct in the graph, though the entire sequence of shots clearly shows alternation.

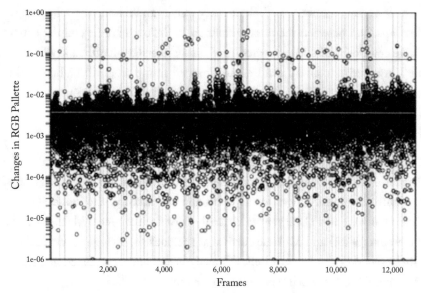

Figure 2.9: **Differences in the Gini values between successive frames in the Bodega Bay sequence.**

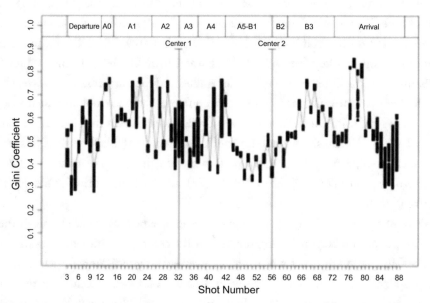

Figure 2.10: **Gini coefficients of each frame broken down by shot number.**

We should note that the RGB graph does not necessarily indicate that there is alternation in the sense of Melanie/dock/Melanie/dock/Melanie. However, one would still be able to say that there is alternation of the RGB pallets, regardless of whether a human viewer would say that the same objects were in front of the lens. Such an RGB alternation might have its own discursive power.

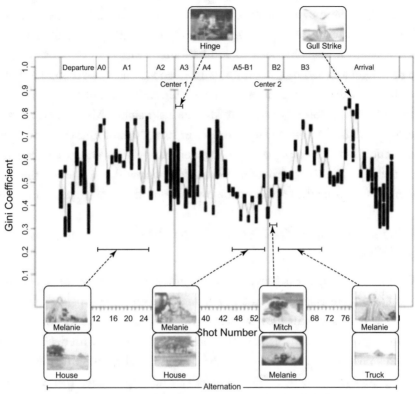

Figure 2.11: "Tact map" showing Bellour's hinge sequence and other key features.

Bellour's hinge sequence runs from frame number 5219 to frame number 6447—Bellour's shot numbers 32–36 (A3). Bellour also refers to this sequence as the first of the two centers. It would make some sense, then, that it would be in the vicinity of the center and the final frame number 6447 is very near the center of 12,803 frames. More significant is the distribution of the Gini values—they are clustered more closely to the .5 line and they display much less variation than we see in most of the rest of the graph. Given the different form of the distributions on either side of the first center it is not untenable to assert the graphic appearance of a hinge (Figure 2.11).

What is not so immediately evident graphically is the second center—that point in the sequence when Mitch sees Melanie—a second center in that it breaks up the rhyme of the trip out and the trip back for a second time. That is, Melanie has exited the house and heads back to the dock and the boat. It seems that after having been in the house—the first center—Melanie will simply head back; however, Mitch's discovery of Melanie and the eventual uniting of "hero and heroine for the first time in the ironic and ravishing complicity of an exchange" (Bellour, 1969, p. 53) interrupt the return.

Although Bellour suggests that the second center "stands out less starkly," it does nonetheless stand out. Shot 43, whose large number of Gini values suggests both its length and the varying data set, is where Melanie moves along the dock and into the boat. Shots 44 and 45 begin the pattern of displacement along the Gini value that was typical in the earlier alternation. This alternation pattern develops strongly between 48 and 54—alternating Gini values remain almost fixed in place along the Gini axis and they occupy a narrow band of the axis. At 55, the shot crosses the 0.5 boundary and the subsequent Gini values suggest alternation again, though of a more widely distributed sort. It is during this fragment that Melanie has watched Mitch, then, at 54 Mitch runs to the house and at 55 Melanie stands up and tries to start the motor. The second center displays a form of alternation, but this takes place in a manner that presents almost a mirror image of the alternation in the trip out—the alternation here hanging below the .5 line. As the second center closes, the alternation repeats the pattern of the trip out—all the Gini values arcing above .5.

2.4.11   DISCUSSION OF STRUCTURE ANALYSIS OF BODEGA BAY   ·
SEQUENCE

The order of magnitude difference between the mean differences for key frames and non-key frames presents a numerical representation of the key frame tact. We have a precise, numerical way of speaking of the key frames identified by Bellour, as well as an automated way of detecting them.

The clustering of Gini coefficients in the "on water" sequences with distinctly different and separated patterns presents a numerical representation of the alternation tact. Melanie's Brenner house sequence presents a distinctly different numerical and graphical representation, giving us the hinge tact. The numerical and graphical "bunching up" in the representation of Mitch's discovery of Melanie and their double seeing alternation, presents us with the second center and a means for speaking precisely of the two-centers tact.

Bellour does not speak to any significant degree about the gull strike on Melanie, though the strike is often mentioned in other discussions of the Bodega Bay sequence. The entire strike is approximately one second of running time and may have been too microscopic for Bellour to address in his analysis. However, the numerical analysis and graphical presentation present a striking data set. Almost every frame presents a Gini value significantly different from its predecessor. This is a very high entropy portion of the sequence—several rapid changes in the data stream in less than a second of running time is a very different pattern from that of any other portion of the film. We suggest that digital precision might have enabled Bellour to speak of this fragment.

In some sense, the hardest thing about what we are doing is seeing what is actually computable only from the physically present data. That is, film criticism and analysis have so long depended on human engagement with the physical document that the distinction between the data stream of the document and the contribution of the viewer's prior knowledge of what is represented remain difficult to tease apart. So we can easily cluster shots with roughly similar RGB patterns. However, going from an MS of Melanie in the boat to an LS of Brenner's house, while it shows us an RGB change does not show us anything that would definitively indicate MS to LS. Also, one could imagine a change from MS to LS (say a cityscape of one or two building fronts to a LS of several buildings) in which the RGB would remain fairly constant. Within any one film or one director's body of work we might be able to make some calculations that would describe/predict CS MS LS changes, but there is just nothing inherent only in the data that makes that a widespread property. This problem does not diminish either Bellour's analysis or the digital analysis—it simply speaks to the complexity of understanding filmic documents and even simply describing them accurately. Indeed, this demonstrates one of our initial assertions: that the engineering of the message structure and the semantic meaning are separate, complementary notions.

That said, the close correlation between the frame-to-frame analysis and Bellour's writing suggests that our use of an expert analyst's response to *The Birds* indeed demonstrates the validity of this approach to numerical and graphical representation of filmic structure. Perhaps one of the most significant consequences of the close correlation is the availability of a vocabulary for description and analysis. A fundamental problem with previous systems of analysis has been the reliance on words to describe visual, time-varying documents. Being able to represent visual attributes and time-varying states of the attributes at the pixel, frame, frame set ("shot"), sequence, and document level with the same processes and terms should enable deeper and more fruitful analysis.

At the same time, the techniques provide means for discovering structural elements. It would be too facile to suggest that we now have a robust mechanism for automated description of filmic structure; however, we do at least have a robust automated means for mapping the structure. We could run any film through a frame by frame comparison of RGB and be able to state that certain portions remain stable for some time, then change; and at some points, rapid changes take place—the points of change, the points of discontinuity in the data stream, represent points where something different is happening.

Perhaps even more intriguing and a likely avenue of rewarding research would be the use of RGB fingerprints in classification. Do all of Hitchcock's films, or at least those from a particular period, share the same fingerprint patterns? If De Palma is the heir to Hitchcock, do his films actually bear a numerical similarity to Hitchcock's films? Do music videos and early Russian documentaries (for example, Vertov's (2002) *Man with the Movie Camera*), films with very different structures from the classic Hollywood films studied by Bellour, yield useful numerical descriptions?

Of course, most moving image documents are made up of more than simply RGB data. Multiple sound tracks for voice, narration, sound effects and music significantly increase the amount of data available for analysis; however, there is no reason that these time-varying data could not be described using a similar numerical and graphical technique.

As we have demonstrated here, the data available for analysis is not limited to the signals available in the physically present document. Bellour's analysis of *The Birds*, in essence, becomes another signal or memetic attribute of the document. Other critics who have commented on *The*

Birds or viewer reactions to the piece could be analyzed in the same manner that we have applied to Bellour's work. Every person who interacts with a document and commits some permanent behavioral product of that interaction contributes to the document's signal set for subsequent uses.

Considered from our perspective, this contribution becomes a fundamental aspect of the setting for considering the relationship between the document/message structure and the semantic meaning. The additional signal, for example a review, can have a significant impact on whether a document is accessed and on how it is evaluated for fitness to a given information need. The document is not necessarily static with the same impact on any given user; rather, it is an evolutionary process. The concept of document as evolutionary process receives more discussion in Anderson (2006) and Wilson (1968).

Bellour sought means to explore and represent moving image documents with the precision already applied to verbal documents at the micro and macro levels. He sought means to go beyond what Augst (1980b) termed the "gratuitousness and arbitrariness of impressionistic criticism." The digital environment offers the opportunity to do so; to enable speaking directly of the native elements such as the RGB components and their changes across time; and, to paraphrase Godard, to confront vague ideas with precise images.

2.5   STORY FIVE: WHAT MAKES A MOVIE AND WHY DOES IT MATTER?

Movies do not move. Essentially all movie formats are made up of still images displayed rapidly. Each of the 16 mm frames to the left is about the size of a fingernail. In projection, a frame is held motionless, a shutter opens and allows light to pass through and project an image onto a screen, the shutter closes, another frame is pulled into place, the shutter opens, … 24 times per second. The process of intermittent motion was the invention of the Lumiére brothers in 1895.

Electronic, analog, and digital formats, while they do not present still images observable by the naked eye, do store data in single frame packets. The frame has been the addressable unit of the movie since the earliest of days. The frame is a still photograph, so a movie can be said to be a collection of still photographs. What makes a movie is something more than viewing a collection of still images.

We opened this lecture with two quotes from highly regarded filmmakers and directors:

The dominant, all-powerful factor of the film image is rhythm, expressing the course of time within the frame.

Andrey Tarkovsky (1987), *Sculpting in Time*

Shot and montage are the basic elements of cinema. Montage has been established by the Soviet film as the nerve of cinema. To determine the nature of montage is to solve the specific problem of cinema.

Sergei Eisenstein (1969), "A Dialectic Approach to Film Form," in *Film Form*

We did so in order to point out the fundamental role of movement at the frame level as the primary component of moving image documents. At the same time, the two quotes bespeak a fundamental rift in thinking about what sort of movement counts and how it ought to be achieved. Should we to essentially leave the camera alone while making long recordings of action in front of the lens, as Tarkovsky argues, or should we to construct movement (and meaning) by placing a variety of images together in rapid succession as Eisenstein argues? We argue that the controversy is essentially a tokenizing issue—looking at the issue of movement from a macro level. Looking at change of the video signal over time at the pixel level essentially resolves the issue.

The frame has been the fundamental unit of production of movies, enabling control of the viewing experience down to the fraction of a second. Eisenstein and Vertov and most editors working in analog film made mechanical cuts at the frame lines; digital editors work with pixels and timelines, but still cut at the frame level. The frame serves as a robust means of sampling the movie data stream and an explanation of what is a movie.

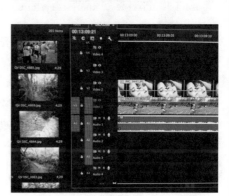

Figure 2.12: **Above**: top left, Eisenstein edits; right, later analog editing. **Lower**: left, mechanical frame level editing mechanism; right digital frame level editing.

For some time we have been examining ways to describe filmic documents in unambiguous ways, to describe the structure of a movie, to compare structures of movies, and to engineer a robust model of moving image documents. We had made significant progress toward these goals combining the idea of seeing moving image documents as signal sets together with what might broadly be called a behavioral component. This behavioral component consisted in the well-established semiotic literature, particularly Metz, Bellour, and Augst; and the theories and practices of behavior analysis.

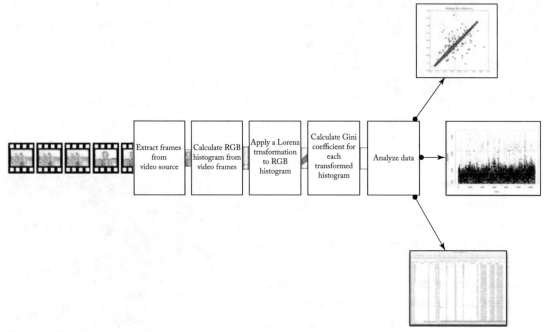

Figure 2.13: Pixel level analysis system.

Our first step was to step away from the debates and failures inherent in seeing the "shot" as the unit of analysis. As Bonitzer (1977) notes, the definition of "shot" is: "endlessly bifurcated," essentially rendering the shot useless as a unit of analysis. We used changes in the red, green, and blue components of every pixel in every frame of a film sequence to find points of discontinuity in a film. By itself, this approach is interesting but does not provide any particular way to find significant points of discontinuity. Bellour had wrestled for some time with the notions of how films generate meaning; he, too, looked to significant points of discontinuity in the signal set. In his work on the Bodega Bay sequence from Hitchcock's *The Birds* he used his highly regarded critical expertise to determine the significant points of discontinuity. We used Bellour's approach to develop a computational heuristic for description of any film—we assumed he was engaging a signal set and characteristics of the signal made it possible for him/necessary for him to see points of discontinuity.

Our efforts replicated Bellour's work very well and we validated the Bellourian heuristic with our analysis of Looney Tunes films by two different directors. The work with our heuristic met with enthusiasm from film theorists and documentalists (e.g., Buckland in *Document (Re)turn: Anderson, O'Connor, and Kearns provide a striking example of combining radically different qualitative and quantitative analytical methods in their discussion of the [Bodega Bay] sequence of Hitchcock's The Birds* (Skare and Lund, 2007, p. 319)).

Still, a heuristic is of only limited value for defining "moving image document" and describing films in a manner useful for classification. Our current challenge is to engage more films and push beyond a heuristic. We currently have RGB signal data for the frames of 60 filmic documents—Hollywood titles, experimental of various sorts, TREC (Text Retrieval Conference) test documents, animations, TV shows, etc.

Briefly, we use the same sort of signal data acquisition as in our previous work, we simply use a different form of analysis. We derived RGB values for each frame (1,800 frames per minute); posited an even distribution (as per Gini analysis); derived the area between the RGB histogram and the line of even distribution; for each and every pair of frames we subtracted the derived area for frame n from the derived area for frame $n + 1$. Plotting the differences yielded a graphical representation of structure, particularly points of discontinuity.

A seemingly simple shift of perspective provides another way to look at the frame- to-frame change. If we plot the same data on a Cartesian plane with value for frame *n* as the X-coordinate and the value for frame $n + 1$ as the Y-coordinate, we have a system in which the unit of analysis is the CHANGE—this depends on the pixel level data stream (actually sub-pixel as R, G, B).

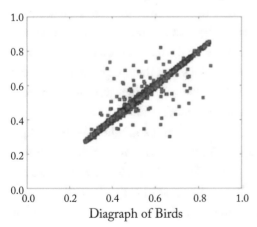
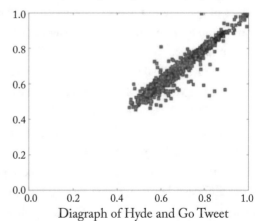

Diagraph of Birds   Diagraph of Hyde and Go Tweet

Figure 2.14: Digraphs of a feature film and a Looney Tune cartoon.

Presenting our data in this digraphic way allows us to see a structural pattern within an entire film. The greater the deviation of a plotted point for any frame pair from the norm, the greater the probability that pair bounds a point of significant discontinuity. In examining data with digraph we see the same frame pairs data as in our previous method, but we see them more obviously. Also, we now have the means of constructing a formula for what constitutes a movie—most frames would have to lie along the line, some would have to lie off the line. The art and craft of movie making, and a way of characterizing filmic structure, lies in how many lie off the line and by how much.

Significance of points of discontinuity can be presented and examined in two ways. With Bellour we have significance defined by a recognized expert in his expert subjective viewing. With empirical data derived from RGB values and shown to be consistent with Bellour's expert notion of consistency, we can define significance (on the whole and with some intriguing exceptions) to be any plotted point of change falling outside one standard deviation. With diagraphic presentation of RGB data and a much larger set of filmic documents, we have gone from heuristic to the algorithmic. We can take this same data and present it in a rather different form—*synthetic frames*. It is not too facile to say that each plotted dot in the digraph is roughly equivalent to a synthetic frame.

The data for just those pixels that are different between frame N1 and frame N2 can be used to generate a viewable image that is neither of the two frames nor is it made up of some regions of one and some regions of the other; in other words, it is synthetic. In most movies there are periods where most of the frames are similar, although not exactly alike; then there is some significant change. In our frames from *The Birds* we see Melanie in a boat for several seconds, then we see the farmhouse she is approaching, then we see her in the boat again. In the theatrical release of the *The Birds* there were 24 frames for each second of viewing time, so in a sequence of four seconds length we would see 96 frames of Melanie in the boat. Not much changes from frame to frame, but there are some changes from frame to frame; the boat is in slightly choppy water, so the woman and the boat have slightly different distances from the frame edges. These small differences yield what almost looks like a pencil sketch of just the major outlines, since the watercolor remains the same, the boat color remains the same, the hair color remains the same, and the coat color remains the same—they just shift a bit from frame to frame. Timing is in standard format of hours: minutes: seconds: frames.

When we reach the point of change from Melanie in the boat to the farmhouse—frame X_{last} (00:01:03:15) and Y_{first} (00:01:03:16), as one might expect, there are many more points of difference so the synthetic frame shows many more points than the sketched outline. Then, once we are at the difference between frame Y_{first} (00:01:03:16) and Y_{second} (00:01:03:17) the synthetic frame is made up of only a few points of difference; although the camera has the point of view of the woman in the boat and the boat moves, there are small shifts from frame to frame.

What is it then that distinguishes a movie from a static still photograph or a set of static still photographs, as in a slideshow? The narrow constraints that provide the viewer of the document the illusion of motion and a sense of narrative in the broadest sense make the distinction. There is a narrow window of entropy necessary for maintaining the illusion of motion; too much entropy and the document loses coherence, while too little entropy and the document no longer engages the viewer.

Figure 2.15: Synthetic frames showing small frame to frame variation (above) and large (below).

We need a little more though. The illusion of motion is normally brought about by the slight changes in data from frame to frame when played back at the intended or nominal speed of the medium. A viewer of a collection of random photographs could arrange a set of prints or digital files and allot a set time period for viewing each image and set an order in which they would be viewed, but this would not necessarily present any perception of motion, nor would it necessarily be considered a representation of motion. It would be, essentially, a slide show; it might have thematic coherence, yet would not be a moving image document.

For another case to consider, we turn to a recent development in video to find a transitional case—the Ken Burns effect. Documentarian Ken Burns developed a technique by which "Action is given to still photographs by slowly zooming in on subjects of interest and panning from one subject to another." The illusion of motion is generated by moving the camera (or software version of a camera) over the image, thus producing a set of frames that have the sort of difference between any two consecutive frames we discussed above. The image on the screen, the stimulus set to the eyes of a viewer, is changing at a standard rate; the illusion of motion though is motion of the still photograph rather than of the objects in front of the original camera. Here a sample of frames from two seconds of panning to the left across an image of a city street.

This is not necessarily a cheat in terms of message making or story telling and the effect does depend on the same persistence of vision that seems to account for what would normally be called a movie, yet there is no illusion of motion in the ordinary sense of some objects moving against a static backdrop and with regard to one another. We are speaking here of message making, of a filmmaker coding a message; as Blair [Hayes too sort of] suggests, the filmmaker dances with the viewer, making assumptions about the viewer's decoding abilities. Persistence of vision sets limits on coding practices; it frames the rate of change in the visual data stream at playback. Too little change from frame to frame and the viewer perceives no motion; too much change from frame to frame and the ability to merge the data is lost.

Any single pixel address within a frame is comprised of four values: red, green, blue, and opacity—RGBA or RGBα. For any pair of frames two additional values are added to the pixel address data: directionality and magnitude. These form a vector describing the amount of change over time; in a movie this period is now ordinarily 1/30th of a second.

So what? We assert that the meaning of a video document—of any document—is its functionality for the author and its functionality for any viewer. Any document is structured data (coded data). Movies present movement. In order to analyze movies to understand how they are coded to generate meaning and, at the same time, to develop methods of categorizing movies based on their coding structures—what might be called fingerprinting—we need to be able to describe movement in rigorous terms. We need to be able to describe and compare sorts of motion without losing sight of the motion. In order to facilitate retrieval and understanding of moving image texts we have to come to grips with the precarious balance between stillness and movement we encounter at every step. Ultimately, it is the transit from one still image to another which has defeated every attempt to freeze the film-text as it turns into something else—a still photograph if you stop the machine, or any number of quasi-cinematic representations if you slow it down or speed it up. Yet, it remains, in Bellour's term, unattainable in motion—"le texte introuvable."

CHAPTER 3

Coda: Provocations on Filmic Retrieval, Hunting, Meandering, and Browsing

3.1 HOW ARE WE TO FIND AND MAKE SENSE OF FILMIC DOCUMENTS?

The meaning of a moving image document is bound up in its structure. Tarkovsky and Eisenstein have very different notions of structure, yet both make films that work. We developed a suite of analysis tools to enable close structural analysis of the time-varying signal set of a movie. We take an information theoretic approach—message is a signal set—generated (coded) under various antecedents—sent over some channel—decoded under some other set of antecedents. Cultural, technical, and personal antecedents might favor certain message making systems over others; the same holds at a recipient end—yet, the signal set remains the signal set. Starting with Hitchcock, moving through Looney Tunes and numerous feature films, and fine-tuning with Warhol and Vertov, we honed ways to provide pixel level analysis, forms of clustering, and precise descriptions of what parts of a signal influence viewer behavior. These can be used across critical platforms.

We do not make a distinction between analysis of structure and retrieval; if content is retrieved by any means, knowing the structure can help determine if the content will be meaningful to an individual seeker and if content requires hunting, having topographical maps can aid that hunting.

3.1.1 RETRIEVAL MAY NOT BE A SUFFICIENT TERM

Retrieval scarcely covers the range of scenarios of finding and using filmic documents, as it is derived from 15th century French roots meaning "to find again" such as when a hunting dog finds lost game. Retrieval implies that a document has been discovered/described (cataloged/indexed) and that when a party seeking useful information comes to the system, the document can be found again. We have been speaking structural analysis rather than "retrieval" in order to provide tools for finding useful filmic information; to provide means for understanding documents; to provide ways of finding one's way in a collection of filmic documents. It is relatively easy to do a search for a feature film or television program or documentary on a particular topic by using words, yet it is not so simple to find filmic documents that will fit individual preferences for style, to sift through hours and hours of footage seeking a particular scene or look, to browse a collection in order to "shake up the knowledge store" (Overhage and Harmon, 1965).

Retrieval of word-based documents—their description and the description of question states that would be satisfied by them—is by no means a simple matter, yet the fact that the documents, their descriptions, and the questions ordinarily put to retrieval systems all use words provides a simplifying framework. Extracting native elements (words) and comparing them is a substantial starting point.

Describing word-based documents is founded on understanding the structure of such documents. Since many searches are for objects or concepts, it is useful to know the difference between nouns and verbs or adjectives when describing the documents or constructing a query; distributions of words across a text as well as co-occurrences also give clues to probability of satisfaction.

3.1.2   PREDICAMENT OF CATEGORIES

We can look at searching for a document as attempting to describe or find a class that holds both the seeker's knowledge state and some documents (representations of knowledge states of authors) in the expectation that some of the attributes of some of the documents will fill in the empty cells of the matrix of the seeker's knowledge state. At least with words we can use definitions, synonyms and antonyms as preliminary tools for finding a class of documents with some probability of satisfying a request. Even with word-based documents the process is fraught with well-known difficulties. Predicting what class will hold the request and some useful documents depends in part on whether the question is well-articulated and satisfiable by particular documents, whether the question state is known but a likely class of documents is difficult to describe, or whether the question state is wide open, as in meandering or browsing, in which case an entire document collection becomes the set of documents to be examined in the search for satisfaction.

Even under the best of circumstances, Wilson cautions:

> *Unless indexing is done specifically for me, and on the basis of intimate knowledge of my interests and requirements, it is likely that I shall always have to engage in exploration, in searching, for the things that are most important to me. Indeed, in any but the hypothetically completely exhaustive "concept bibliography," we may find it necessary to explore, or search, for things that have not been collected or arranged or identified in a fashion that suits our purposes.*

(Wilson, 1968, p. 101)

3.2   WHAT THEN OF MOVING IMAGE DOCUMENTS?

Greisdorf and O'Connor (2002) demonstrated a wide range of responses in a simple experiment of putting a set of pictures into categories—different terms for the same object in an image, different levels of generality (landscape with horse and rider or cowboy, e.g.), and different categorical assumptions (cookie with food or with tire, ferris wheel, and other round objects, etc.).

Augst and O'Connor (1999, p. 345) asserted about filmic documents:

> *Mechanism has posed a major barrier to user control over locus of insertion, depth of penetration, and [duration] of engagement. For decades, the film scholar sat in a dark room and watched the serial unrolling of the text. Sometimes this was in a theater where no control over the text was available; sometimes this was in a room with a projector that could be stopped, reversed, slowed, speeded up. In each case, however, the engagement required serial viewing. Even the scholar with access to film production equipment or later, videotape, could not escape the serial nature of the engagement.*

They note also, quoting promotional material for an early video digitizing system: "…the ability to jump anywhere on digital video still won't help you find where to jump (p. 348).

3.3   WAY POINTS FOR HUNTING, BROWSING, AND MEANDERING

> *Perhaps when the conditions of film projection will change, through technical progresses which promise to allow us to have access at will to films, it may become possible to walk leisurely, to wander, to loaf about, stroll and loiter … delighted to explore the ordered depth of a film, to appreciate a thousand details in a sequence while experiencing the unique character of the whole.*

> Baudry (1980)

> *Many people today think tracking is simply finding a trail and following it to the animal that made it. I think the true meaning of reading tracks and signs in the forest has been pushed into the background by an overemphasis on finding the next track… If you spend half an hour finding the next track, you may have learned a lot about finding the next track but not much about the animal. If you spend time learning about the animal and its ways, you may be able to find the next track without looking. . . . Tracking an animal… brings you closer to it in perception.*

> Rezendes (1992)

> *The Meander River (Anatolia, Turkey) once formed a crucial conduit for Mediterranean trade and traffic between Europe, North Africa, and Asia. At its mouth sat the foremost Aegean port city Miletus, acclaimed for the origins of Greek philosophy and science. Historians Herodotus*

and Strabo mention the Meander's winding ways, which were so striking that "meander" came to mean riverine sinuosity and to stand for anything twisting and curving. The geomorphological process of meandering is as intricate, twisting, and turning as the curving Meander River. A meandering river takes time while it covers a broad area, scouring the hardest rock, depositing the quickest sands. It is deeply spatial, temporal, and specific—continually finding its trajectory, while making it. It is profoundly responsive to the lay of the land, the nature of the climate, the character of human interventions, and a multitude of other vectors.

Meandering privileges exploration: a messy process, with stumbling, learning from failures, following contingent relations, a going back and forth. Meandering foregrounds the searching in the notion of re-search. It invokes a model of engineering in terms of ingenuity, a bricolage and tinkering that acknowledges and interacts with various kinds of knowledge and expertise, that is capable of adjusting itself to local situations and demands, instead of simply following the straight lines of rule-driven reasoning.

The Meander confounded early lawyers concerned with boundaries and scientists concerned with the mechanisms of meandering streams. Meander symbolized irregularity, complexity, ambiguity, and instability. In the latter part of the twentieth century precisely these 'meandering' qualities brought out the value of multiple perspectives in arts and sciences; the weak ontology of becoming became as valuable as the traditionally more privileged strong ontology of being; the inductive, analogical, and emergent as valuable as control and generalizability (O'Connor and Copeland 2003: 99). The understanding of probability and complexity provided new forms of explanation and new ways to operate even within fields long founded on 'ideal' characteristics and laws.

Klaver (2014)

Among the initial reasons for conducting research on the structure of filmic documents was browsing, as described by O'Connor:

The value of a broad notion of browsing and the consequent utility of a surrogate which facilitates the inspection of the collection in a variety of ways is suggested in a number of areas. Bates and Arnheim both posit a playing with concepts freed from the cause-effect of the external world, as well as from the linear constraints of language. Cadbury and Poague, in considering aesthetic experience, posit a "consciousness we have attending to our exploratory behavior when we don't mean to use it and results guide action rather than the action of continuing to explore it." (Cadbury and Poague, Film Criticism: A counter theory, *p. 276) Similarly, Leide refers to Koestler on creativity, particularly the activity of "homo ludens" deriving a "eureka response" from the convergence of parallel thoughts on different planes. This recalls the quote regarding 'free play with concepts and the description of concept building as the recurring of the same picture in*

many series of 'memory pictures' described by Einstein. (Houltn On Scientific Thinking p. 380)
This in turn recalls Pryluck and Arnheim on the imbedded meaning of moving image documents,
in part, by the sequencing of images "ambiguous precisely as a consequence of their specificity."'

Pryluck (1976,) and Arnheim (1974, p. 246)

We look at our model as something of a topographic map showing the terrain of a filmic document—here meaning a small number of frames, an entire production, a collection of productions, and all the derivative films such as trailers, reviews, and fan re-edits. Such a map may serve as a guide to a particular film, as a picture of the lay of the land of similar filmic documents, or as an orienteering or exploring map suggesting possible paths and features but no particular target or goal.

We share Mamber's notion of providing spatial and visual access points—indeed O'Connor and Augst produced a digital interface to *The Birds* not dissimilar from Mamber's. Both interfaces have the appearance of influence from Bellour's analysis of key frames in the Bodega Bay sequence from the film. The key frames were "eyeballed" so the work was tedious and, more importantly, subject to flaws of human interpretation. Bellour and Mamber both rely on "the shot" as the unit of measure and the unit of meaning. This is not a fundamental problem so long as one is dealing only with classic Hollywood narrative films; however, once one steps out of that realm changes in the data stream can occur without well-defined markers of change. Even within Hitchcock's *The Birds* the entry of the sea gull that strikes the heroine is not marked for change at the frame when the gull actually appears or the frame in which it actually exits. Rorvig noted that NASA was once wrestling with the problem of how to analyze long-take data streams of space exploration with as many as two dozen cameras running continuously how many eyes would it take to look at hours of almost the same scene watching for the first sign of a crack in a hull or (as he joked) the three frames with little green aliens waving (Rorvig, Personal Communication, 1999).

There is a fundamental problem with the "shot"—the definition is "endlessly bifurcated" in Bonitzer's terms. There is no universally applicable standard of just how long a shot is, what defines its beginning and end, or how much should be contained within a shot. This is why we look at the data stream and its changes over time at the pixel level. This is where analysis of viewer reactions to stimuli and providing tools for finding and understanding overlap.

3.4   PROVOCATIONS

At the time of O'Connor's initial research in the early 1980s there were no print catalogs of documentary or educational films that had even one frame from each and every film in the catalog. Today, images derived from videos abound in web-based interfaces to collections of films. Here we have just two samples to raise the issue of "just where to jump." The issue is nowhere near so vexing as it was in the days of analog film prints, when simply acquiring a print and threading it into a projector were enormously time consuming compared to clicking on a YouTube or Vimeo link and seeing within seconds whether or not the document is likely to be satisfactory. Still the "where to jump" issue has not entirely disappeared in a world of billions of videos.

The frames in the Vimeo interface (Figure 3.1) were automatically extracted from a default point in each piece approximately 1/10th of the playing time of the whole document. Thus, the frame for *Strong CityXP720* comes a few minutes into the piece originally made to run 28 minutes on television, following establishing shots of the rodeo grounds and the rodeo parade. The frame from Practice is from less than one minute into the seven-minute piece, following an abstract sequence of one gymnast then a title card. The frame from *Horse Pulling* is from the first image frames of the film, but the film is a video duplicate of a 16 mm print and has all the leader material including the countdown numbers and the title card. All the frames representing videos in the YouTube interface are simply the middle frames of each respective piece. How one is to know just what is in the frames on either side of the interface frames is unknown, unshown.

Strong CityXP720
Brian O'Connor | 2plays

Proximity & Anecdata: Enhancing Understanding of Sch…
Brian O'Connor | 8plays

Scraps
Brian O'Connor | 13 plays

Practice
Brian O'Connor | 119 plays

No Place To Go
Brian O'Connor | 8plays

Running Film
Brian O'Connor | 25 plays

Horse Pulling
Brian O'Connor | 65 plays

Manchester Heartbreak HEVC NOV 20
Brian O'Connor | 189 plays

Figure 3.1: Vimeo interface frames from O'Connor collection.

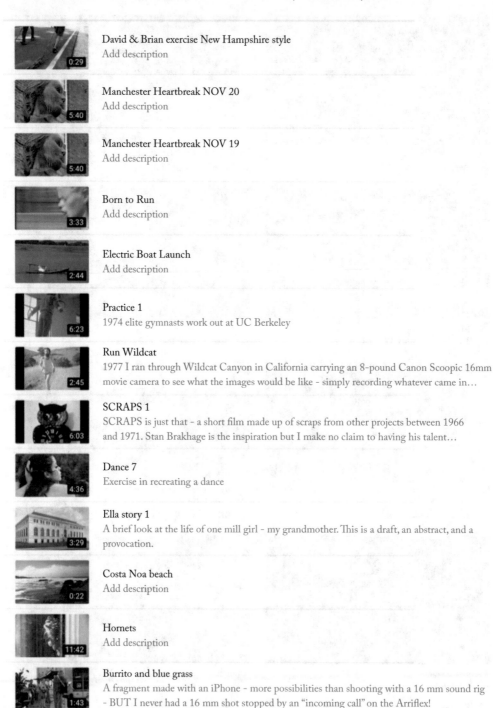

Figure 3.2: YouTube interface frames from O'Connor channel.

3.5   AUTHOR—MESSAGE—RECIPIENT RELATION

In our first modeling of users and makers of documents as fundamentally the same—both representing knowledge states based on their understandings of their environments—we realized that we were being too static. Blending our model with constructs from behaviorism, we worked out a model that could account for differences in time, place, and circumstances. The model could now also account for moving about in time—being able to watch a classic film while understanding that production methods and standards were different; looking at the one existing photo of a grandmother at 10 years old, wishing there had been YouTube videos while knowing there just were not; watching a favorite movie on a tablet late at night, skipping to just the parts that were especially well crafted; examining Riefenstahl's diving sequence to compare it with the Billy Joel "River of Dreams" video. Eventually we removed whatever hints of linearity and parallelism of time or place.

Here we present a small case study to illustrate the author—message—recipient relationship and how structure can foster different meanings.

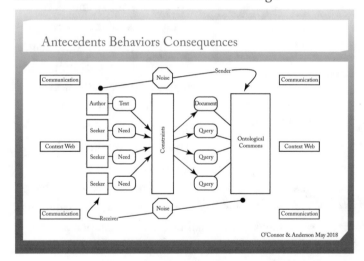

The film *Gymnastics USA* was made in 1976 about the selection for the U.S. Olympic Gymnastics team. There was essentially no narration, largely upbeat music of various genres composed for the film; the editing was "poetic," often blending only portions of routines into collages of human movement reminiscent of the Diving Sequence in Riefenstahl's *Olympia*; there is no indication of leaders, losers, winners. The *International Gymnast* magazine hailed the film as one of the best gymnastics films ever made; the judges for the American Film Festival (the premiere showcase for documentary and educational films at the time) did not even advance it to the final showings because it had "no coherence" and "was obviously made by someone with no understanding of gymnastics or sports in general (in fact the producer was a former world champion gymnast and coach of Olympic gymnasts; the filmmaker was a competitive fencer and long distance runner.) Looking at the qualifications of the two audiences with their two very different meanings one sees participants in the very topic of the film on the one hand and network production staff on the other. Neither is more understanding or more qualified. The film festival judges were looking at structure from a point of view of what had "high production value" and would be of the standard structure for a sports film, while the gymnasts were looking through embodies eyes knowledgeable about the particular sport.

3.6   ADDITIONAL THOUGHTS

Here as a summary and to elicit more conversation about filmic documents are a few of the thoughts from a presentation we made at the Ends of Cinema conference at the Center for 21st Century Studies at the University of Wisconsin, Milwaukee.

3.6.1   FUNCTIONAL ONTOLOGY

Analysis of the signal set across the evolution of film from Edison to Hollywood to Brakhage to cats on social media yields a common ontology with instantiations—responses to changes in coding and decoding antecedents.

> *The functional ontology is the set of environmental stimuli and historical factors that have function for an individual at a particular point in time—those things that select behavior.*
>
> Richard Anderson
> *Doing Things with Information*
>
> O'Connor & Anderson May 2018

The coding and decoding of messages of any sort—grocery list, Rosetta Stone, selfies, dissertation, cavepaintings, lullaby—are profoundly influenced by the physical, cultural, temporal aspects of the environment of the message maker and of the message recipient.

Whether one is watching a movie in an IMAX theater with hundreds of other people or watching the same movie on a small tablet with headphones, one is seeing the same text but having a different experience. Similarly, if one is watching a classic noir feature or a favorite television show from the 1960s on a laptop, time and place can scarcely help but impact the experience, the meaning. The notion of "ends of cinema" rests on the degree to which cinema is defined by the viewing experience. We posited that the genetic makeup of the time-varying signal set of cinema did not change across time and that a functional ontology construct could model differences in reception/perception without an end.

3.6.2   ARROWSMITH ON FILM AND LITERATURE

We make one more nod to Greek and Latin literature, looking to classicist and film scholar William Arrowsmith (1969), whose article "Film as Educator" stands both as a call to applying our best tools to the conduct of the humanities and as a marker for an ontological shift in media habits. Arrowsmith sat in on a class session in which O'Connor was giving a critique of Arrowsmith's book on the satires of Juvenal; in 1982 he was a correspondent on the dissertation research reported here.

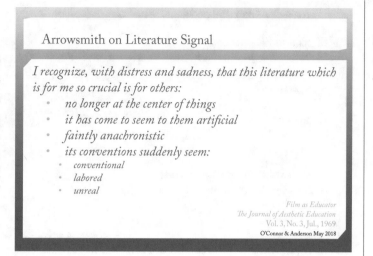

Arrowsmith on Literature Signal

I recognize, with distress and sadness, that this literature which is for me so crucial is for others:
- *no longer at the center of things*
- *it has come to seem to them artificial*
- *faintly anachronistic*
- *its conventions suddenly seem:*
  - *conventional*
  - *labored*
  - *unreal*

Film as Educator
The Journal of Aesthetic Education
Vol. 3, No. 3, Jul., 1969
O'Connor & Anderson May 2018

3.6.3   BERTRAND AUGST

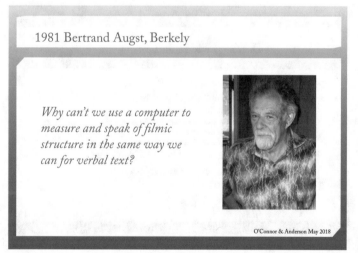

1981 Bertrand Augst, Berkely

Why can't we use a computer to measure and speak of filmic structure in the same way we can for verbal text?

O'Connor & Anderson May 2018

It is impossible to overstate our gratitude for Bertrand Augst's contributions to our work and to film studies as a whole

During the late 1960s and early 1970s, UC Berkeley film theorist Bertrand Augst had made computer-generated concordances of Baudelaire, Mallararmé, Rimbaud, Lautréamont, Apollinaire, Saint-John Perce, Proust, and Du Côté de chez Swann. It was of little wonder then that he would ask why we could not do the same for films. In 1981 there was simply no way to digitize films. So we set about modeling and doing some early pre-tests. We dropped the literary metaphor (a shot is like a sentence or a paragraph,) we replaced vague concepts such as Long Shot and Close Up with percentage of pixels within an area of the frame, we devised the multi-threaded time-varying signal set, and we devised some early measures of discontinuity.

3.6.4   SHANNON BINARY SYSTEM

Our approach rests on Claude Shannon's entropy based model of communication and adopts his assertion that message and meaning are distinct—meaning depends on decoding of the message

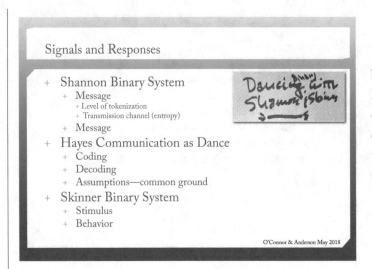

but is not part of the message. Hayes and Blair similarly model communication as a dance of coding and decoding. Skinner too posits a binary system of stimulus and response.

3.6.5   UTILITY OF THE FUNCTIONAL ONTOLOGY MODEL

The functional ontology model accounts for the distinction between message and meaning and the environmental antecedents that yield coding and decoding behaviors. Looking to behavior enables experiments. In Bellour we had an expert whose output we could observe with regard to *The Birds*; we could examine the film signal stimulus for the components that stimulated Bellour to behave as he did—devise his model; then we could compare our results with his expert results.

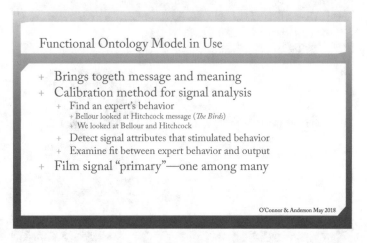

3.6.6   POINTS OF DISCONTINUITY

Significance of Points of Discontinuity

+ With Bellour we have significance defined by a recognized expert's subjective viewing.
+ With empirical data derived from RGB values and shown to be consistent with Bellour's expert notion of consistency, we can define significance (on the whole and with some intriguing exceptions) to be any plotted point of change falling outside one standard deviation.
+ With diagraphic presentation of RGB data and a much larger set of filmic documents, we have gone from heuristic to the algorithmic.
+ We can take this same data and present it in a rather different form—synthetic frames. Each plotted dot in the digraph is roughly equivalent to a synthetic frame.

It ought to be noted again that use of discontinuities for analyzing film is analogous to analysis of word documents. The ability to describe structure of film documents at various levels of analysis and in discipline neutral terms has been demonstrated; now we seek to provoke new challenges and new applications.

3.6.7   MOVIE STIMULI AND EFFECT

So…

+ Stimuli of a movie have behavioral effect on the viewer.
+ Functional ontology model extends to stimuli in viewing environment.
+ Environment of the viewing—the reaction of the crowd to a jump cut, the smell of popcorn, the floor, sticky from spilled soda, the richness of the sound system, friends' opinions, alternate venues—all function to reinforce, punish, or extinguish behavior.

O'Connor & Anderson May 2018

For some the "ends of cinema" refers to the time(s) when changes in technology yielded significant changes in how and where and when movies were shown and viewed. The introduction of air conditioning to theaters, the multiplex, the disappearance of the double feature, drive-ins, television, etc. We posit that the functional ontology model provides a framework for discussing these attributes in much the same way that we can discuss changes in the filmic data set.

3.6.8   MOVIE STIMULI AND EFFECT 2

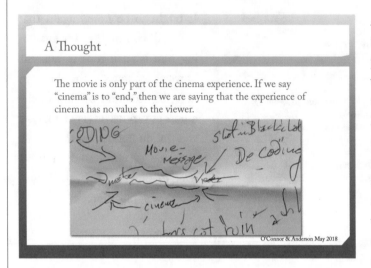

A few additional thoughts came to mind while listening to other presenters. Looking at movies within a "dancing with entropy" model (Kearns and O'Connor, 2004)suggests that the movie itself is only a part of the "cinema" experience. The end of cinema has been predicted frequently in the past—introduction of sound would kill the visual art; introduction of color would do the same; television would take people away from the theater. Even if cinema means large gatherings in front of large screens, the death notice is premature. If home viewing of productions such as *Breaking Bad* and *Game of Thrones* is any indication, smaller groups watching at home can still interact with others over social media in a distributed cinema.

3.6.9   EVOLUTION OF CINEMA

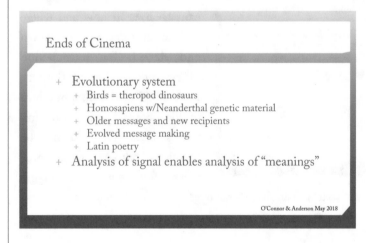

Evolution might be a more useful term than end of cinema. Birds embody the genetic material of dinosaurs; Homosapiens sapiens hold onto Neanderthal genetic material; Catullus' "odi et amo" holds Vergil's Latin poetry genetic material.

3.6.10 THE END

Since it is a tradition of the cinema to announce to the audience "The End," we have done so here. The image behind the words shows the end of O'Connor's neighborhood cinema in the 1950s—the Empire Theater. Yet movies are still produced and shown to audiences large and small; they are still produced by major studios; and they are now produced by independent artists; and they are made by individuals for personal use and publication on social media.

We sought precise, repeatable, numeric, and graphical representations of the film signal that would enable discussion of filmic structure—the message—so that discussions of meaning would have a significant touchstone. It might be said that we sought a method of fingerprinting the frames. It is our passionate hope that this will be the start of discussions, arguments, experiments, and discovery of more and more useful ways to bring filmic documents to the point of use.

Bibliography

Addiego, W. (2005, October 14). Domino quit modeling for the glamour of guns. SFGate.com. Retrieved April 14, 2009, https://www.sfgate.com/movies/article/Domino-quit-modeling-for-the-glamour-of-guns-2564914.php. 38

Anderson, R. (2006). Functional ontology modeling: A pragmatic approach to addressing problems concerning the individual and the informing environment. Unpublished doctoral dissertation. 34, 50

Arnheim, R. (1974). *Visual Thinking*. Berkeley, CA: University of California Press. 63

Arrowsmith, W. (1969). Film as educator. *Journal of Aesthetic Education*, 3(3), 75–83. DOI: 10.2307/3331705. 34, 68

Augst, B. (1980a). Defilement into the look. In: Cha, T. H.K., Ed. *Apparatus: Cinematic Apparatus: Selected Writings*. New York: Tanam Press, pp. 249–59. 17, 26

Augst, B. (1980b). Instructor's course notes on Bellour's "Les Oiseaux: Analyse d'une sequence." 38, 50

Augst, B. and O'Connor, B. C. (1999). No longer a shot in the dark: Engineering a robust environment for film study. *Computers and the Humanities*, 33, 345–63. DOI: 10.1023/A:1002459729916. 37, 61

Austin, J. L. (1976). How to do things with words: The William James lectures, delivered at Harvard University in 1955. Oxford: Clarendon Press. 3

Baudry, J. (1980). Author and analyzable subject. In: Cha, T. H. K., Ed. *Apparatus: Cinematic Apparatus: Selected Writings*. New York: Tanam Press, pp. 67–83. 61

Bellour, R. (1969). Les Oiseaux: Analyse d'une séquence. *Cahiers du Cinéma*, October, p. 216. 38, 41, 47

Bellour R. and Penly, C. (Eds.) (2002). *The Analysis of Film*. Bloomington, IN: University of Indiana Press. 41

Bersani, L. and U. Dutoit. (1998). *Caravaggio's Secrets*. Cambridge, MA: MIT Press. 24

Bonitzer, P. (1977). Here: the notion of the shot and the subject of cinema. *Cahiers du Cinema*, 273, 107–15. 21, 28, 38, 52

Catania, A. C. (1998). *Learning* (4th ed.). Upper Saddle River, NJ: Prentice Hall. 40

Dailianas, A., Allen, R. B., and England, P. (1995). Comparison of automatic video segmentation algorithms. Paper presented at *SPIE Photonics East'95: Integration Issues in LargeCommercial Media Delivery Systems*. DOI: 10.1117/12.229193. 39, 43

Danto, A. C. (1998). Carravagio's Gaze. Review of *Caravaggio's Secrets*, by Leo Bersani and Ulysse Dutoit, Lingua Franca, Fall 1998. 24

Day, W. F. and Leigland, S. (1992). *Radical Behaviorism: Willard Day on Psychology and Philosophy*. Reno, Nev.: Context Press. 40

Eisenstein, S. (1969). *Film Form: Essays in Film Theory*. New York: Harvest Books. 38, 51

Greisdorf, H. and O'Connor, B. (2002). Modelling what users see when they look at images: a cognitive viewpoint. *Journal of Documentation*, 58(2), 6–29. DOI: 10.1108/00220410210425386.

Greisdorf, H. F. and O'Connor, B. C. (2008). *Structures of Image Collections: From Chauvet-Pont-d'Arc to Flickr*. Westport, CT: Libraries Unlimited. 3

Hitchcock, A. (Director). (2000). *The Birds* [Motion picture]. (The Alfred Hitchcock collection). Universal City, CA: Universal Studios Home Video. 38

Holmes, O. W. (1859). The stereoscope and the stereograph. *Atlantic Monthly*, June. 13

Kearns, J. (2005). Clownpants in the classroom? Entropy, humor, and distraction in multimedia instructional materials. Paper presented at *DOCAM 05*, Document Academy. 43

Kearns, J. and O'Connor, B. C. (2004). Dancing with entropy: Form attributes, children, and representation. *Journal of Documentation*, 60(2), 144–63. DOI: 10.1108/00220410410522034. 39, 43, 72

Klaver, I. J. (2018). Meandering and Riversphere: The potential of paradox. In *Open Rivers: Thnking Water, Place & Community*. Issue 11. https://editions.lib.umn.edu/openrivers/article/meandering-and-riversphere-the-potential-of-paradox/. xvii

Klaver, I. J. (2014). Meander[ing] Multiplicity. In *Water Scarcity, Security and Democracy: A Mediterranean Mosaic*. Edited by Francesca de Châtel, Gail Holst-Warhaft and Tammo Steenhuis. Ithaca, NY: Global Partnership Mediterranean, Cornell University and the Atkinson Center for a Sustainable Future. 62

Kodak (1964). *How to Make Good Coaching Movies*. Kodak. 7

LaSalle, M. (2005, October 28). *This Guy Just Can't Hang Up His Mask*. SFGate.com. Retrieved April 14, 2009. 38

Mamber, S. (2002). Space-time mappings as database browsing tools. In: Dorai, C. and Venkatesh, S. (Eds.) *Media Computing*. The Springer International Series in Video Computing, vol 4. Boston, MA: Springer. DOI: 10.1007/978-1-4615-1119-9_3.

Maron, M. E. (1982). Associative search techniques versus probabilistic retrieval models. *Journal of the American Society for Information Science*, 33, 308–10. DOI: 10.1002/asi.4630330510. 17

Metz, C., (1974). *Film Language: A Semiotics of the Cinema*. (M. Taylor, Trans.). Chicago, IL: University of Chicago Press. 18, 39

Nichols, B. (1982). *Ideology of the Image: Social Representation in the Cinema and Other Media*. Bloomington, IN: Indiana University Press, p. 48. 19

Novitz, D. (1977). *Pictures and Their Use in Communication*. The Hague: Nijhoff, p. 17. DOI: 10.1007/978-94-010-1063-4. 18

O'Connor, B. C. (1985). Access to moving image documents: Background concepts and proposals for surrogates for film and video works. *Journal of Documentation*, 4(4), 1985. DOI: 10.1108/eb026781. 17

O'Connor, B. (1991). Selecting key frames of moving image documents: A digital environment for analysis and navigation. *Microcomputers for Information Management*, 8(2). 43

O'Connor, B., Anderson, R., and Kearns, J. (2008). *Doing Thngs with Information: Beyond Indexing and Abstracting*. Westport, CT : Libraries Unlimited. 16

Overhage, C. and Harman, R. (1965). Intrex : Report of a planning conference on information transfer experiments. Cambridge, MA: MIT Press. 60

Peritore, N. P. (1977). Descriptive phenomenology and film: an introduction. *Journal of the University Film Association*, 29, 3–6, 5. 19

Pryluck, C. (1976). *Sources of Meaning in Motion Pictures and Television*. New York: Arno Press. 18, 37, 63

Pryluck, C., Teddlie, C., and Sands R. (1982). Meaning in film/ video: order, time, and ambiguity. *Journal of Broadcasting*, 26, 685–95. DOI: 10.1080/08838158209364037. 18

Rezendes, P. (1992). *Tracking & the art of seeing : how to read animal tracks & signs*. Charlotte, VT: Camden House. 61

Salt, B. (2003). *Film Style and Technology History and Analysis* (2nd ed.), London: Starword. 43

Shannon, C. E. and Weaver, W. (1949). *The Mathematical Theory of Communication*. Urbana, IL: University of Illinois Press. 40, 43

Skare, R. and Lund, N. (2007). *A Document (Re)turn: Contibutions from a Field in Transition*. Frankfurt am Main: Peter Lang. 53

Skinner, B. F. (1953). *Science and Human Behavior*. New York: Macmillan.

Skinner, B. F. (1957). *Verbal Behavior*. New York: Appleton-Century-Crofts. DOI: 10.1037/11256-000. 40

Tarkovsky, A. (1987). *Sculpting in Time: Reflections on the Cinema*. Austin, TX: University of Texas Press. 50

Vertov, D. (1984). *Kino-eye: The writings of Dziga Vertov*. Berkeley, CA: University of California Press. 38

Vertov, D. (2002). *Man with the Movie Camera* [Chelovek kino-apparatom (1929)] [motion picture]. Chatsworth, CA: Image Entertainment. 49

Watt, J. H. (1979). Television form, content attributes, and viewer behavior. In: Voight, M. J. and Hanneman, G. J. (Eds.). *Progress in Communication Sciences, 1*. Norwood, NJ: ABLEX, pp. 51–89. DOI: 10.1002/asi.4630310516. 19, 21

Wilson, P. (1968). Two kinds of power: An essay in bibliographic control. Berkeley, CA: University of California Press. 50, 60

Wittgenstein, L. (1953). *Philosophical Investigations*. New York: Macmillan. 40

Worth, S. (1981). *Studying Visual Communication*. Philadelphia: University of Pennsylvania Press, 1981. DOI: 10.9783/9781512809282. 18, 20, 21

Yamaguchi, K. and Kunii, T. L. (1982). PICCOLO logic for a picture database computer and its implementation. *IEEE Transactions on Computers*, C-31, 1982, 983–96. DOI: 10.1109/TC.1982.1675907. 19

Authors' Biographies

Brian C. O'Connor together with Rich Anderson founded the Visual Thinking Laboratory in The College of Information at the University of North Texas. He holds degrees in Greek and Latin literature, Film Production (Fine Art), and earned his Ph.D. in theory of organization of information at the University of California, Berkeley. He made his first photograph in 1952 and has remained immersed in image making since. He has produced documentaries and art films, has written on photography, chaired several dissertations on various aspects of the use of images, and has recently received the inaugural Teti Research Fellow at the New Hampshire Institute of Art where he studied nineteenth century photographic processes.

Richard L. Anderson is currently Director of Information Security for the University of North Texas System. He has a background and publications in Behavior Analysis and earned his Ph.D. at the University of North Texas doing research on functional ontology construction and the information environment. He is an accomplished photographer, he conducts courses in both photography and cybersecurity, and he mentors doctoral students conducting research in various aspects of information theory.

Printed in the United States
by Baker & Taylor Publisher Services